Praise for *Revolution of Rav Kook*

"Rabbi Schwartz should be congratulated for his important book, which opens the door to the profound thoughts of Rav Kook on such a diverse range of topics. I am certain that this book will be a great blessing to any serious student who speaks English."

— RABBI SHLOMO AVINER, *Rosh Yeshiva, Ateret Yerushalayim; Rabbi of Beit El*

"Rav Kook's words are revolutionary even in this generation. His ideas are so relevant that it's a little bit of a shame that we haven't spread them further. This book has taught me so many ideas that have changed the way I think about the Jewish people. Whoever reads this book will find it life-changing."

— RABBI SAM KASSIN, *Dean and Founder, Shehebar Sephardic Center, Jerusalem*

"Rabbi Schwartz has collected, sorted, ordered, edited, and translated the essential writings of Rav Kook's great creation. This book invites the student to expand and go deeper and deeper into the all-encompassing philosophy of one of the giants of recent generations."

— RABBI DR. YEHUDA BRANDES, *Director, Herzog Academic College*

"Rabbi Schwartz has given expression to Rav Kook's unique ability to contain so many diverse perspectives in one holistic worldview. This book has done an exceptional job of portraying Rav Kook's unique personality."

— RABBI YOCHANAN FRIED, *Chairman, Beit HaRav Kook*

THE SPIRITUAL REVOLUTION OF
RAV KOOK

THE WRITINGS OF A JEWISH MYSTIC

TRANSLATED AND INTRODUCED BY RABBI ARI ZE'EV SCHWARTZ

Copyright © Ari Ze'ev Schwartz
Jerusalem 2018/5778

Excerpts from Simcha Raz, *A Tzaddik in Our Time* (Jerusalem: Feldheim, 1976) and *An Angel among Men: Impressions from the Life of Rav Avraham Yitzchak Hakohen Kook*, trans. Moshe D. Lichtman (Jerusalem: Urim, 2003) are used by permission of the author.

Translations from Moshe Nachmani, *Chai Ro'i* (Jerusalem: Or Ha'orot, 2015) are used by permission of the author.

Translations from Chayim Lifshitz, *Shivchei Reiyah*, 3rd ed. (Beit El: Shilo Birkatz, 2010) are used by permission of the publisher.

Translations from Ran Sarid, ed., *Chadarav*, 3rd ed. (Ramat Gan: Dabri Shir, 2008) are used by permission of the editor.

Cover Design: Jacob Schwartz
Typesetting: Raphaël Freeman, Renana Typesetting

If you have any questions, please email
Rabbi Ari Ze'ev Schwartz: contact@arizeev.com
To find out more about Rabbi Schwartz's spiritual center,
https://www.facebook.com/IndependentSpirituality

ISBN: 978-965-229-913-0

5 7 9 8 6

Gefen Publishing House Ltd.
6 Hatzvi Street
Jerusalem 94386, Israel

972-2-538-0247

Gefen Books
c/o 3PLCenter
3003 Woodbridge Ave.
Edison, NJ 08837
516-593-1234

orders@gefenpublishing.com
www.gefenpublishing.com

Printed in Israel

* * *

Library of Congress Cataloging-in-Publication Data

Names: Kook, Abraham Isaac, 1865-1935. | Schwartz, Ari Ze'ev, translator.
Title: The spiritual revolution of Rav Kook: the writings of a Jewish mystic / translated and introduced by Rabbi Ari Ze'ev Schwartz.
Description: Springfield, NJ : Gefen Publishing House, [2017]
Identifiers: LCCN 2016052863 | ISBN 9789652299130
Subjects: LCSH: Kook, Abraham Isaac, 1865-1935. | Judaism--Philosophy.
Classification: LCC BM755.K66 A3 2017 | DDC 296.8/32092--dc23
LC record available at https://lccn.loc.gov/2016052863

To Tzofia Leah and Yael Hadar
May Rav Kook's wisdom illuminate your lives as much as it has mine.

Contents

Foreword by Rabbi Dr. Yoel Bin-Nun — ix
Preface — xi
Abbreviations — xviii
Introduction — 1
The Four-Part Song — 7

THE FIRST SONG: THE SONG OF THE INDIVIDUAL

1 The Individual — 11
2 Torah — 25
3 God — 39
4 The Meaning of Life — 51
5 *Teshuvah* and Personal Growth — 57
6 Character Traits — 67
7 Listening to the Inner Child — 79
8 Prayer — 85
9 The Spiritual Importance of Creativity — 99

THE SECOND SONG: THE SONG OF THE NATION

10 Ethics and Concern for Others — 115

11 Zionism — 125
12 The Holiness of the Body — 143

THE THIRD SONG: THE SONG OF HUMANITY

13 Faith and Science — 155
14 Liberal and Progressive Values — 165
15 Relationship to Other Religions — 177

THE FOURTH SONG: THE SONG OF CREATION

16 Animal Rights and Vegetarianism — 187

UNITING THE FOUR SONGS

17 Rav Kook's Own Inner World — 199

POSTSCRIPT

A Spiritual Letter to the Reader — 221
Meet Rav Kook — 239
Acknowledgments — 267
About the Author — 269

Foreword by Rabbi Dr. Yoel Bin-Nun

RAV KOOK ONCE WROTE, "THERE ARE THREE LEVELS THAT THE individual and collective perfection of the Jewish people must be based on: a return to physicality, a return to humanistic morality, and a return to the source of the nation. True holiness can only come about through the combination of all three qualities" (SK 3:63).

There are those who have found in Rav Kook the revival of the Jewish nation. They see Rav Kook's unique attitude toward the pioneers who built up the land of Israel, whom he desired to draw close with affection even when they rebelled against Torah and mitzvot.

There are those who have found in Rav Kook the inner "I," the uniqueness of each individual soul. There are also those who have found in Rav Kook the renewal of *halachah*, and who have seen the combination of natural and humanistic ethics with holy morality. There are those who have understood kabbalah, those who have searched for philosophy, and those who have found the combination of both in Rav Kook's unique personality.

In Rabbi Ari Ze'ev Schwartz's own powerful personal exploration, he was amazed to discover the many faces and diverse teachings of Rav Kook, all of which were drawn from the light of one single soul that yearned for a holistic perspective. "God is one and His name is one" (Zechariah 14:9).

RABBI DR. YOEL BIN-NUN is one of the founding heads of Gush Emunim, Yeshivat Har Etzion, and Herzog College for Teachers. He is behind the revolution of Tanach study in the land of Israel. In addition, Rabbi Bin-Nun was one of the paratroopers who liberated the Old City in the Six-Day War, an unofficial advisor to Prime Minister Yitzhak Rabin, and one of the main characters in Yossi Klein Halevi's popular book *Like Dreamers*.

Preface

"It Is Forbidden to Study Rav Kook"

I was born in Sydney, Australia, and grew up in a very Zionist home. My parents met in Israel on a kibbutz. I went to a religious Zionist school, and my family even moved to Israel for a year and a half when I was six years old. Hebrew was a secret language my family would use when they didn't want other people to know what we were talking about. My grandfather was the great-grandson of Rabbi Shmuel Mohilever, one of the head founders of the Religious Zionist movement. Zionism is in my soul.

After I finished high school, I began studying music and film. I felt increasingly empty and directionless. Two years into my studies, I took a trip to Israel and decided to begin studying in a *charedi* (ultra-Orthodox) yeshiva in Jerusalem. I studied Talmud, *halachah*, musar, kabbalah, and Jewish philosophy. I completely immersed myself in spirituality. I would stay up until two in the morning studying Jewish texts, meditate for an hour each day, and spend my time talking to kabbalists. I felt I had finally found meaning and purpose.

Strangely enough, despite the fact that I was living in Jerusalem, the heart of Israel, Zionism was never spoken about. Yom Ha'atzmaut and Yom Yerushalayim were not celebrated. I remember going up to one of the heads of the yeshiva to ask him if we could learn Rav Kook. He looked at me with a serious face and replied, "Rav Kook isn't one of our *gedolim* [leaders]; his ideas are very dangerous, and it is forbidden to study his books."

This intrigued me. What were these ideas that he considered so dangerous?

The Misrepresentation of Rav Kook

When I was growing up, I of course knew the name of Rav Kook. I knew a handful of things about him too: that he was a Zionist rabbi, that he was the first modern-day chief rabbi of the land of Israel, that he had a passionate love of the land of Israel, and that he supported Zionism even though it was led by secular Jews. And as I would find out later, this is as much as most people know about him. For many Jews, Rav Kook is simply a cliché symbol of Zionism.

Yet, the more I studied the writings of Rav Kook, the more surprised I was to discover how distorted this image is. Rav Shlomo Aviner, one of the top experts on the writings of Rav Kook, has said that only 10 percent of Rav Kook's writings focus on Zionism. Almost 90 percent of what Rav Kook wrote has no reference to Zionism at all.[1] The topics that interested him were the individual person's search for meaning, using Torah as a means to discover one's own unique soul, developing one's understanding of God, personal growth, the relationship of faith with science, creativity, animal rights, and much, much more. In other words, the more I read of Rav Kook's own words, the more I understood just how misrepresented and misunderstood Rav Kook is.

Let it be clear, I am not saying that Rav Kook's relationship to Zionism isn't important or significant. It is. And I have included an entire chapter in this book on Rav Kook's Zionistic writings. Nevertheless, in order to truly understand the spiritual revolution of Rav

---

1. For more on this topic, see Rav Aviner's lecture "Is Rav Kook Still Relevant Today?" which can be found on his website, filled with many fascinating lectures about Rav Kook, at http://www.ateretmedia.org/ra_sic/5770_5774/ra_sic_7006 27.mp3.

Kook, one has to encounter the many faces of Rav Kook. In fact, this is the reason the front cover of this book has so many pictures of Rav Kook on it. The idea is to restore a more accurate and authentic understanding of Rav Kook, to show all his faces, all the different aspects that make up this unique figure.

The Disappearance of Rav Kook

I often ask my students if they have ever heard of Rav Kook. "Of course," they respond. I then ask them if they have ever seen a photo of Rav Kook. "Many times," they answer. But when I ask them if they have ever learned a paragraph of Rav Kook's own words, too often the answer is "Never." I remember one student even telling me that he had been to a "Machaneh Rav Kook" (Rav Kook camp) where no words of Rav Kook were studied or mentioned.

Indeed, as I have come to realize over the years, only a small number of people study Rav Kook's actual writings. Most *charedi* people don't study Rav Kook because he is "too Zionistic." Many secular Zionists don't study Rav Kook because he is "too religious." A large number of Reform and Conservative Jews don't study Rav Kook because he is associated with right-wing politics and the settler movement. And surprisingly, even many religious Zionists don't study Rav Kook because they say his Hebrew is too poetic and his ideas too abstract.

And therefore, it seems that Rav Kook has become one of the most famous thinkers in Jewish history, and yet also one of the least studied thinkers in Jewish history. This book is an effort to introduce you to Rav Kook on a personal level, to inspire and challenge you with his wisdom.

I once spoke in front of a crowd of a hundred Jewish youth leaders from all over the world on the topic of ideology. I asked them, if they were to teach a class on their favorite topic in Judaism right now, what would they teach? The room was silent. I then asked, if they were to introduce me to their favorite music or sport right now, what would they say? Immediately hands went up, and the common theme to the passionate responses was that they were about *someone*. Being passionate about a musician or athlete and resonating on a personal level with that individual enhanced the passion for the music or sport itself. In the same way, I believe students need to rediscover our Jewish intellectual and spiritual role models so that we can build a more personal connection with Judaism.

A Personal Challenge

Over the last seven years I have been teaching Rav Kook to young men and women who have chosen to learn for a year in Israel between high school and university. I will never forget that at the end of my first year of teaching, a student came up to me to say how much he had loved learning Rav Kook's writings. He asked how he could continue learning them when he went back home. I walked him over to a bookstore to help him find an appropriate book.

In front of us was a selection of Hebrew and English books of Rav Kook's writings. After picking up one of the Hebrew books, he said, "Rav Ari, do you really think I will have enough time next year to sit down and translate Rav Kook's words into English so that I can learn them? It's hard enough learning it with you." I picked up an English book to give him. After opening it and reading several paragraphs, he looked at me and said, "I didn't understand anything." He found the ideas to be too abstract and the language too lofty. Unfortunately, the student went back to America without a book.

This was my dilemma seven years ago, when considering how to help my students develop an independent relationship with Rav Kook's writings. Either the Hebrew is too hard – advanced even for a native Hebrew speaker, all the more so for someone not fluent in the language – or the English is too lofty due to its literal translation of the already poetic Hebrew. Ever since then, I have been writing this book. I did not know it would be a book; at first I thought it would be a few translations that I could send to my students. But eventually, I found that I had translated enough to compile a book that I believe represents many of the most significant pieces of Rav Kook's philosophy.

The Unique Writing Style of Rav Kook

Those who have tried to learn Rav Kook's works in Hebrew know how difficult his language and sentence structure are. When Rav Kook first arrived in Israel, he had a dream of writing a series of books. *Eder Hayakar* (1905), and *Ikvei Hatzon* (1906) were the only two books that he actually wrote. After being constantly criticized by editors for not writing in a professional and orderly way, Rav Kook eventually came to the realization that the rules of essay writing were too limiting for his unique style of writing. Giving up the dream of writing books, he confined himself thereafter to short entries in his diary. This became his favorite way of expressing himself. From these short paragraphs, his son, Rav Tzvi Yehuda Kook, and his student, "the Nazir," compiled most of the books that exist today under Rav Kook's name.

I have tried my hardest to stay true to the actual words of Rav Kook without being so literal that the ideas become incomprehensible when translated. This can often be rather difficult. There have been times when I have spent over an hour on a single sentence, trying to translate the deep and flowery words into a clear and succinct sentence in English.

When Ibn Tibbon first attempted to translate the Rambam's famous philosophical book, *Guide for the Perplexed*, from Arabic into Hebrew, he wrote a letter to the Rambam asking for advice. The Rambam wrote back the following:

> I want to teach you an important principle: any person who desires to translate from one language to another, and tries to translate each word exactly and keep the same sentence structure, will exert much effort, yet the translation will be vague and unclear.

Do not do this. Instead, a translator must first try to understand the meaning of the sentence, and only afterwards try to articulate it in the target language. Certainly, this is impossible to do without changing the order of the sentence, using a few words to translate one word, translating many words with one word, leaving out words and adding words until eventually the meaning of the sentence will be understood clearly in the new language.

This is what wise people should do when translating. May God help them and increase their reward." (*Igrot Harambam* [Maaleh Adumim: Shilat, 1995], p. 532, my own translation)

Commentary versus No Commentary

I started writing a sentence-by-sentence commentary on the pieces included in this book many times, but each time I would stop as I considered that this would take the focus away from Rav Kook's own words and place it on the commentary instead. There have been many valiant efforts to create commentaries on Rav Kook, and I in no way want to diminish their successes. Nevertheless, my personal goal is to introduce my students to Rav Kook's own words with as little distraction as possible.

As a sort of compromise between allowing people to read Rav Kook's actual writings and helping them to understand his difficult ideas, I have broken up long paragraphs and inserted headings to hint to the reader what Rav Kook is communicating in each piece. These headings are meant to serve as a subtle form of guidance without taking away from the focus on Rav Kook's words.

In addition, I have written brief introductory essays to each chapter to suggest to the reader what questions and problems Rav Kook will be addressing in that collection of writings. One of the unique things about the way Rav Kook wrote is that each piece is usually very short and to the point. Rather than having to work through a long essay in order to understand the main message, you will find that

Rav Kook simply tells you what he thinks at the very beginning. This structure of writing is very enjoyable to learn, as one can simply open up the book in one's free time and read a short and inspirational idea.

Who is this book written for? On the one hand, it is written for myself. As a rabbi and teacher, I have slowly begun to realize that only ideas that come from an inner place of authenticity have the power to transform others. It is not enough to simply communicate information to people; spiritual concepts are hollow when they aren't drawn from a sincere drive for self-discovery. Studying Rav Kook's writings has truly opened my mind and heart to a new way of perceiving the world; I am not the same person I was before I began writing this book.

On the other hand, this book is written for my students. According to authentic Jewish consciousness, the ultimate goal is not only individual enlightenment. There is a world full of pain and suffering, and it is the task of a Jew to be a ray of light in a galaxy of darkness. To be a part of the spiritual revolution of Rav Kook, is to be involved in a lifelong mission of transforming one's soul, one's people, and eventually, the entire world.

I truly believe that there is a magical quality in Rav Kook's writings that has the ability to bring together many different faces. This is not an abstract theory. Many times, I have publicized a class I was giving on Rav Kook, and to my pleasant surprise, the people who have showed up have been as diverse as *charedi*, secular, religious Zionist, and even non-Jewish. Indeed, there is something undeniable about the ideas Rav Kook wrote down.

But why take my word for it?

It is my tremendous honor to share with you the spiritual revolution of Rav Kook. May this book be a blessing for all who read it. I know that it has been a blessing in my life.

With love and respect,

Rabbi Ari Ze'ev Schwartz
Jerusalem, 2017

Abbreviations

AT – *Arpelei Tohar*
C – *Chadarav*
CT – *Chazon Hatzimchonut v'Hashalom*
EA – *Ein Aya*
KYK – *Kevatzim Miktav Yad Kodsho*
IR – *Igrot Hare'iyah*
MA – *Musar Avicha*
MaR – *Maamarei Hare'iyah*
MiR – *Middot Hare'iyah*
MoR – *Moadei Hare'iyah*
MS – *Midbar Shur*
O – *Orot*
OE – *Orot Ha'emunah*
OK – *Orot Hakodesh*
OR – *Olat Hare'iyah*
OT – *Orot Hatorah*
OTf – *Orot Hatefillah*
OTs – *Orot Hateshuvah*
PR – *Pinkasei Hare'iyah*
SK – *Shmoneh Kevatzim*
SR – *Shivchei Hare'iyah*

Introduction

BEFORE WE START THIS SPIRITUAL JOURNEY OF STUDYING THE writings of Rav Kook, it is important to remind ourselves of the educational goals that Rav Kook is trying to achieve with his writing.

Rav Kook says that he wants to inspire and awaken an inner transformation in the lives of his readers.

> I feel a push from within to talk about *teshuvah* (spiritual transformation).... I must help our generation understand its depth and guide us to actualize it in our individual and collective lives. (OT, introduction)

In other words, Rav Kook is not writing simply to describe and define an abstract idea; rather, he is deliberately trying to affect the inner thoughts and emotions of the reader. In order to do this, Rav Kook believes that his writings must not only be true, but also creative, beautiful, and inspiring to read.

> The beautiful and profound emotions of *teshuvah* must be revealed though creative writing. This is in order that our revolutionary generation will understand *teshuvah* in the depths of their souls in a new and fresh way. People will come back to Judaism and be healed. (OT 17.5)

When we read the writings of Rav Kook, therefore, we must bring both our intellects and emotions to the text; we must come with a mood of openness. Indeed, the goal is that something deep and transformative will happen to us while reading these words.

Rav Kook says that the spiritual goal of studying a text is not only to receive a new idea, but also to awaken to one's own internal divine wisdom. The text must be seen as a tool toward understanding oneself.

> **It is not the goal of any external influence – whether from holy or secular sources – to silence one's spirit and to mute one's independent thoughts. Rather, external information should provide inspiration that one is able to internalize into one's independent self. And through this process, one's own thoughts will develop and become empowered. (OK 1, p. 67)**

For Rav Kook, studying a text must not be a passive experience; rather, there must be an author-reader interaction.[1] Many times, Rav Kook will present his reader with two or three different spiritual paths and then allow the person to decide which path fits best for his or her unique soul. Is your soul more drawn to individual meaning or nationalism? Are you more practical or philosophical and mystical? Are you excited by the uniqueness of the Jewish people or by the divine image in all of humanity? Rather than choosing which is the correct path, Rav Kook will write in a way that will encourage each reader to be actively involved in deciding which path resonates.

In much of Rav Kook's writing, there is a unique author-reader dialogue: the role of the author is to begin the discussion of an idea, yet it is the reader's responsibility to respond by searching for individual personal meaning.

> **Any form of listening must be used as a tool to build the inner self. The center of the Torah is each individual's personal line. This is**

---

1. To read more about the importance of author-reader interaction in Rav Kook's writings, see Dov Schwartz, *The Religious Genius in Rabbi Kook's Thought: National "Saint"?* trans. Edward Levin (Brighton, MA: Academic Studies Press, 2015), pp. 18, 22, 28, 29, 157.

what we will be judged on. This is the most profound question. This is our heaviest responsibility. (OK 3, p. 139)

The text is a trigger, an invitation to clarify one's own inner thoughts; the reader must not only receive from the author but also bring his own insights to the text. And so, when we study Rav Kook's writings, we must recognize that the goal is not only to understand Rav Kook's ideas, but also to understand our own ideas. Through immersing ourselves in his words, we will become immersed in our own deepest thoughts and emotions.

The way Rav Kook wrote down most of his ideas was out of a spontaneous moment of inspiration; he wanted his reader to sense the authenticity and aliveness of his thoughts and emotions.

> I have been overcome by an inner desire to publish some of my diary entries in their original form.... How many pages will it be? I don't know. I only hope that these words, just as they are, without any form of editing, will be a blessing. In fact, perhaps their blessing will be manifested specifically through the lack of editing. "Like warm bread taken on the day of baking" (1 Shmuel 21:7). (IR 2, pp. 292–93)

In many ways, writing was a form of self-discovery for Rav Kook; he too was amazed by the ideas that flowed from his pen.

> It is a very important thing to watch one's thoughts and imagination, and to write down every idea as soon as it is born in the depths of the soul. (SK 8:52)

While it may be possible to work out a systematic structure to Rav Kook's thinking – and many rabbis and academics have indeed tried to do just this – it seems that the most authentic way of reading Rav Kook's writings is each piece on its own.[2] In other words, just as each

---

2. Dov Schwartz has tried to argue that Rav Kook's writings do not strive for sys-

piece was an honest expression of what Rav Kook was thinking or feeling at that very moment, so too, we must approach each piece as its own entity, with its own unique insight and energy. One of the ways to do this is by reading a single piece and then stopping to ponder its meaning before moving on to the next piece. Rav Kook's writings do not read like a structured book with a clear goal from beginning to end. We must learn to appreciate Rav Kook's unique way of writing; we must try to encounter each piece on its own, allowing his honesty and aliveness to affect us.

> I want to pour out my soul in whatever form it takes... we must send out words full of life. (IR 1, p. 267)

And lastly, it is important to remind ourselves that Rav Kook's ultimate goal in spreading his teachings was never to create strict followers, but to unite diverse groups of people.

> If I wished, I could attract a group of followers (who would be considered my Chasidim), to myself who would spread my teachings and thoughts. But I do not want to restrict myself in such a way. I want to connect to the entire Jewish people, and in no way do I desire to be disconnected from any person. (MoR, p. 170)

In a time when there is so much division between religious and secular, right-wing and left-wing, Rav Kook's writings have a major role to play in bringing people together.

The writings in this book are structured based on Rav Kook's piece "The Four-Part Song." This is Rav Kook's spiritual manifesto. It describes four types of people who each sing a different song of

---

temization and even anticipate the postmodern spirit. See, D. Schwartz, *Religious Zionism between Logic and Messianism* (Tel Aviv, 1999), 198233 [Hebrew]; see also J. Garb, "Rabbi Kook – National Thinker or a Mystic Poet," *Daat* 54 (2004): 69–96 [Hebrew].

spirituality; Rav Kook then challenges us to unite them into one unified symphony.

- The first song is the song of the individual; corresponding to this are writings on a personal connection to one's own soul, Torah, God, the meaning of life, spiritual growth, character traits, the inner child, prayer, and creativity.
- The second song is the song of the nation; corresponding to this are writings on ethics, Zionism, and the holiness of the body.
- The third song is the song of humanity; corresponding to this are writings on faith and science, liberal and progressive values, and the relationship to other religions.
- The fourth and final song is the song of creation; corresponding to this are writings on animal rights and vegetarianism.
- At the end of "The Four-Part Song," Rav Kook encourages his reader to unite all four of these songs into one person; corresponding to this are Rav Kook's writings about himself and his own attempts to embody all four of these spiritual values.

Perhaps this is one of Rav Kook's most attractive qualities: he has created a language of inclusive spirituality. He encourages an attitude toward life that isn't about boxing oneself into a specific label, but rather validating and combining all the beautiful qualities of one's soul.

This is the spiritual revolution of Rav Kook.

The Four-Part Song

There is one who sings the song of the individual soul. This person finds everything inside the soul and experiences in it total spiritual fulfillment.

Then there is one who sings the song of the nation, leaving the boundaries of the individual soul, which are found to be too narrow and not idealistic enough. This person yearns for great heights and unites with the entire Jewish people with a deep love. Pained by the nation's sufferings, finding happiness in its dreams, the one who sings the song of the nation is immersed in deep thoughts concerning its past and future, and tries to understand its inner spiritual nature with love and a wise heart.

Then there is one whose soul is so all-encompassing that it expands beyond the limits of the Jewish people: the one who sings the song of humanity. This person's spirit ascends and becomes concerned with the greatness of mankind and its divine image, seeking humanity's ultimate purpose and looking forward to its ultimate perfection. From this source of life, the singer of the song of humanity draws all thoughts and insights, ideals and visions.

Then there is one who rises even higher to unite with the entire world, with all creatures, and with all of existence. And with all of them, the singer of the song of all existence sings. This is a person who is immersed in Perek Shira each day, who is guaranteed the world to come.

And then there is one who rises up with all these songs together. Each gives its voice. Each plays its melody: the song of the soul, the song of the nation, the song of humanity, and the song of existence. All harmonize within the ideal human being at every moment and at all times. (OK 2, pp. 444–45)

The First Song
The Song of the Individual

1

The Individual

"When we forget the individual soul, when we stop paying attention to the inner life of a person, everything becomes confusing and unclear."

MANY SEE RELIGION AS A WORLD OF CONFORMITY. ONE IS COMmanded to pray the same prayers as one's neighbor, to eat the same food, to observe the same festivals, to obey the same laws as everyone else. Indeed, does not the central principle of every monotheistic religion imply that "one God fits all"?

Yet in the modern era, people are no longer interested in a life of obedience and submission. People are seeking out a personal and unique way of living. The "I" is our generation's most prized possession, and we are not willing to give it up for some antique tradition of our ancestors. If religion can only offer us conformity, we feel, then we would best look elsewhere for spiritual meaning. No wonder Buddhism and other practices that focus on individual enlightenment have become so attractive to our generation.

There is truth and necessity in the sense of collective belonging to the Jewish people, but when the individual does not find self-expression, our community becomes one of ghosts.

In this chapter, Rav Kook will describe to us the supreme importance of the individual's role in Judaism.

Being True to Oneself

The World Has Forgotten Its Inner Self

When we forget the individual soul, when we stop paying attention to the inner life of a person, everything becomes confusing and unclear. Therefore, the beginning of *teshuvah* (spiritual growth)... is the return to oneself, to the Source of one's soul. Returning to oneself leads one to immediately return to God, to the Soul of souls; in this way one will grow higher and higher in holiness and purity.

This principle is true for the transformation of the individual, the nation, humanity, and all of existence. All destruction comes about only because we have forgotten and ignored the self. In fact, if a person expresses a desire to return to God, but is not interested in focusing on the self, then this is a fake and deceitful type of *teshuvah*, through which one takes the name of God in vain.

Therefore, only in the great truth of returning to oneself will the individual, the nation, humanity, and all of existence return to its Creator, to the Light of life. This is the secret of the light of the Mashiach – that in his illumination, the entire world will return to its Source. (SK 8:213)

The Root of All Sin: Ignoring Oneself

"I am in the depths of exile" (Yechezkel 1:1). This refers to the inner, essential "I" – whether individual or collective....

"Both we and our forefathers have sinned" (Tehillim 106:6). This hints to the sin of Adam Harishon, who became alienated from his essence. He conformed to the opinion of the snake and thus lost himself. He could not clearly answer the question *"Ayeka?"* (Where are you? [Bereishit 3:9]), because he did not know himself, for he had lost his true "I." He had bowed to a foreign god.

And this was the sin of Israel, who was "seduced by foreign gods" (Devarim 31:16, referencing the sin of the golden calf). She abandoned her essential "I." "Israel ignored goodness" (Hoshea 8:3)....

And so the world continues, descending into the destruction of every "I" – of the individual and of the collective. Expert teachers come and focus on the superficial. They too distract their students' awareness from the "I."

They add straw to the fire, give vinegar to the thirsty, and fill minds and hearts with everything that is impersonal to them. And little by little, the "I" becomes forgotten. And when there is no "I," there is no "He," and how much more so is there no "You."

[The Mashiach is called] "the breath of our nostrils, the anointed one of God" (Eicha 4:20). This is his strength and great beauty – that he is not external to us. He is the breath of our nostrils. We will seek Hashem our God and David our king. We will be in awe of God and His Goodness.

We will seek our "I." We will search for our essence – and discover. Remove all foreign Gods, remove every strange and illegitimate one. *And then you will know that I am Hashem your God, Who takes you out of the land of Egypt to be your God. I am Hashem* (paraphrase of Shemot 6:7).[1] (OK 3, pp. 140–41)

We Have Neglected the Individual

It is impossible for us to speak about a national revolution if we do not first speak about the revolution of each unique individual. In fact, the neglected revolution of the individual soul is what is truly holding us back from a national revolution. (O, "Yisrael" 7.17)

The Problem with Nationalism

There are two problems with nationalism that need to be fixed in order for it to perfect itself.

The first is that nationalism does not focus enough on the individ-

---

1. To help me translate this difficult piece, I relied on Yaacov David Shulman's translation for guidance. It can be found on his comprehensive website of Rav Kook translations: http://www.ravkook.net/souls.html.

ual. Now, since the individual often has great physical and spiritual needs, things begin to go wrong when they are not fulfilled, and the nation loses its strength.

The second problem is that nationalism only focuses on the physical world. But the soul is fulfilled through finding a bridge between the physical and spiritual worlds. In order for this to happen, nationalism must be open to being influenced by spirituality and philosophy. (SK 1:650)

Perfecting the World through Perfecting Oneself
The ideal perfection of a person can only be accomplished by focusing one's energy on improving one's own individual self as much as possible. Yet at the very same time a person should always keep in mind that one's own individual perfection will never be completed until the Jewish people have successfully reached national perfection. And from national perfection, a person must aspire to the perfection of all humanity.

Yet one must be careful never to allow one's desire to improve the masses to undermine the perfection of one's own individual character traits and actions. (EA, *Berachot* 1, p. 47)

First Find Yourself
Individuals must find themselves in themselves, and only after this can one find oneself in the world.

The community must find itself in itself, and only after this can it find itself in all of humanity.

Humanity must find itself in itself, and only after this can it find itself in the entire world. (SK 8:41)

The Exhaustion of Conforming to the Masses
There are certain righteous people who, despite having very spiritual character traits, feel anxiety and pressure within their souls. They

do not focus enough attention on their inner greatness; they do not really believe in the holiness of their desires. As a consequence, they are not aware of the incredible light contained in their thoughts. They walk around bent over, with the weight of the world and its cruel anger hovering above them. They suffer immense spiritual pain. All the narrow-minded thoughts of the masses exhaust their spirits, and they find themselves lacking any strength to elevate themselves to the full height of their own thoughts and desires.

Eventually, they will be forced to release themselves and wake up from this mental slumber. And despite all the peace and respect they give to the ways of the masses, they must return to God, Who is always revealed to them through their own unique windows. (SK 8:6)

Individual and Universal Transformation Are Connected
The more a person engages in self-transformation, the more the world is thereby transformed. (SK 1:454)

Education and the Individual Self

When Education Distracts One from Oneself
Spiritual ideas come to build up each person in his or her own unique way. Any form of listening must be used as a tool to build the inner self. The center of the Torah is each individual's personal line. This is what we will be judged on. This is the most profound question. This is our heaviest responsibility.

There are some people who have opened their ears so wide that they have lost their inner focus. They know many names; only their own names they have forgotten and no longer recognize.

Consequently, all of their effort is for nothing. They have no other choice but to cover their ears in order to block out anything external. Only after this traumatic destruction of going deaf can they return and be renewed. (OK 3, p. 139)

Indoctrination versus Education

It is not the goal of any external influence – whether from holy or secular sources – to silence one's spirit and to mute one's independent thoughts. Rather, external information should provide inspiration that one is able to internalize into one's independent self. And through this process, one's own thoughts will develop and become empowered.

A person drained by a feeling of laziness begins to think that the aim of all external information is to disprove one's thoughts, to crush and to confuse them. As a consequence of this type of thinking, a person feels short-tempered and lacks the motivation for growth.

Indeed, the holy and the secular do influence your spirit. However, when you integrate them, your inner self is enriched. (OK 1, p. 67)

Both religious and secular people were attracted to Rav Kook's unique spiritual teachings. Here is Rav Kook teaching a class at his yeshiva in Jerusalem.

Understanding Oneself

Understanding oneself is the highest level of spirituality. As a rule, anything a person learns is always extracted from the outside world. This is in contrast to one's thoughts, which come to a person from the depths of one's soul. Everything we learn from the outside world must only be seen as a tool for reaching down into the hidden heart, the depths of the soul, the inner logic of one's own wisdom. (SK 5:281)

Lack of Interest in Expert Learning

The great spiritual people discover inside themselves a resistance to being expert learners, since everything is already alive inside them.... They must focus their time uncovering the depths of their own souls. For such people, learning should simply function as an external helper and nothing more. The main source that will lead them to spiritual transformation must be their own inner Torah. "And in his [own] Torah a person should meditate day and night" (Tehillim 1:2).

However, sometimes one does not recognize one's own worth, and focuses on other people's relationship to Torah. One then decides that one must become an expert learner. It is at that moment that these great spiritual souls descend into darkness. (SK 2:172)

The Power of the Soul

Every person has the ability to change the world. It all exists within one's spiritual resources. It all depends on whether or not one has the power to reveal it. Indeed, this is true not only for the sophisticated and knowledgeable, but even the simplest person. There is no limit to the power of the soul. It is a candle of the Divine in the world. (SK 1:846)

The Demanding Soul

The soul's demands point us to where a treasure of life is waiting. Thus, the happiness of a person is dependent on the ability to pay attention to these demands. This principle is true even when the soul is giving off vague noises, when it is impossible to recognize letters, words, rules, or explicit messages. One must gather up these pearls from the ocean of life; and as time continues, with the help of Torah, hidden seeds will sprout into beautiful flowers that are filled with the profoundest resources of vitality. A person will be able to eat from them and live forever. (SK 8:56)

Each Person Is Different and Unique

Each Person Is Called Upon in a Unique Way

All people must understand that they are being called to serve in a way that is unique to their intellectual and emotional personalities, according to each person's unique root soul.

In this world, which includes infinite worlds, one must find the treasure chest of one's life. Do not allow external things that come into your world to confuse you; they will not be absorbed correctly, and you will not be able to gather them into your unique life. Those external worlds will find what they need in order to reach perfection on their own.... You must focus on your own life, on your inner world that fills all that you do. "Each person is obligated to say, 'The world was created for me'" (*Sanhedrin* 37a).

This great level of humility brings joy and helps each person reach the ultimate perfection that is waiting for him or her. Indeed, when one walks down this secure path, one's own unique trail, in a way of righteousness that is unique to oneself, one is filled with the strength of life and the joy of spirituality. The light of God will shine upon such a person, and strength and light will come from one's special letter in the Torah. (SK 4:6)

Stable Souls versus Up-and-Down Souls

God created some people to be straightforward. Their personalities are peaceful. The life of convention and inner stability is their inheritance. Certainly, if they exert themselves in Torah, morals, and wisdom, they will grow to respected heights. Nevertheless, they will always remain people of convention, decent and well grounded. The fate of these people is to be immersed in practical work, or at least practical wisdoms. Their moral standards and behavior are simple and hold up on their own. They may never ascend to the highest, most sublime levels, but they also will not descend to the lowly abyss of chaos.

However, there is a second personality type. These people never have any rest. They are always in a state of drama: either they are ascending to the sublime heights of heaven or they are descending to the bitter depths of disaster. These people need to concentrate on spiritual growth every single day. Such people, when they have discovered ways of life that suit them, will ascend higher and higher. On the other hand, if they neglect their personal paths, they will most likely collapse and descend lower and lower. These people need to be immersed constantly in Torah and self-improvement, ethics, and sacred emotions. And God forbid that they should live a life of conventional work and practical knowledge.

As history progresses, we sometimes find generations that fit into the first personality type; their general personality is stable and calm. The correct education for them is the same as that of the stable individual. On the other hand, there are generations that fit into the dramatic and erratic personality. For them, constant spiritual guidance is required. Sometimes we find people or generations with elements of stability as well as elements of drama and unsteadiness. The leaders, who are concerned with the struggles of the generation, must take care to educate groups and individuals appropriately according to each element. (OK 3, pp. 126–27)

Practical People and Spiritual People

Just as practical people, those who have talents in practical actions and practical wisdoms, are unable to obtain a complete clarity in spiritual matters..., so too, spiritual people are unable to completely understand practical matters....

Nevertheless, there is a type of capacity in the truly spiritual souls to contain everything. But this is only true in the context of the prophecy of *aspaklariya meira* (undimmed clarity). Therefore, only in reference to Moshe was it said, "There was a king in Yeshurun" (Devarim 33:5). But as history progressed, a king and a prophet were separate entities. (SK 1:192)

Specializing Soul versus Unifying Soul

People are not all the same in their spiritual growth. There is a type of person whose spiritual essence is expressed by focusing and specializing on one thing at a time. The more such a person concentrates the mind, learning, understanding, and emotions in a specific way, the more complete and perfected this person will feel.

However, there is another type of person whose spiritual essence is expressed through the quality of diversity. In all important issues, this person feels forced to spread out his or her thoughts and feelings; "from afar they bring their bread" (Mishlei 31:14).

Then there are people who have both of these qualities. They feel drawn toward specialization as well as diversity. When the time of focus rules them, they cannot tolerate any form of diversity; at other times, the quality of diversity reveals itself, and they are unable to bear any type of focus. This principle is true of entire nations. It is the hidden secret of the way the world is run; it is the cause of history and all the different time periods of creation, existence, building, destruction, innovation, and transformation. (SK 5:49)

Don't Hide Your Unique Personality

One should not be discouraged when one sees that one is not able to focus and specialize in one specific field. This is true whether one is not able to go into depth and develop one topic, one attitude, or one singular type of learning. Sometimes one has a unique personality trait that causes one to be attracted to reaching for the unknown, and unifying diverse topics. This type of person should recognize that this is his or her spiritual mission. One should therefore rejoice in one's unique talents. (SK 5:153)

Each Soul Must Give and Receive

For the most part, an individual does not possess a wide array of talents. This is because each unique talent is built on specific personality traits that contradict other traits, and so a person cannot be gifted with them all. For example, a person with a great memory does not necessarily have an introspective mind; and a person who has an introspective mind often lacks the ability to remember many things at once. Or take a poetic person who has tremendous talents in music; he or she may not be capable of understanding practical wisdoms such as engineering or machines. And the opposite is also true: a person who has a great mind for numbers and mathematics often cannot ascend to the heights of music...

So too, there are people who have a natural desire for connecting to God through mitzvot that are directly focused on God (*bein adam la'Makom*), while they may not strongly desire to be involved in mitzvot that are directed toward ethics (*bein adam l'chavero*). Conversely, there are some people who are excited to be immersed in mitzvot that are ethically centered (*bein adam l'chavero*), yet mitzvot that are God centered (*bein adam la'Makom*) and the holiness of faith may not be as strong inside them. In fact, that same natural strength in one's soul that drives a person toward poetry and music is what motivates a person to be involved in spirituality and the honor of God.

This is the great pain that exists in the world: there are strengths and talents that are scattered and contradictory. Nevertheless, the path of truth, which is the path of God, requires each individual to be strong and confident in his or her own talents, and at the same time to honor and respect the talents of others. Each person should desire to influence friends and be influenced by them for the increase of good.... It is through the combining of different talents within each individual that a society is formed. (KYK 1, Pinkas Rishon l'Yaffo 67)

Your Unique Connection to God Energizes You

> "'A song of David; protect my soul, for I am a Chasid' (Tehillim 86:2). This is what King David said before God: 'Master of the world, am I not a Chasid? All the kings of the East and the West sleep until the third hour of the day [late in the morning], but I rise at midnight to give thanks to You.'" (*Berachot* 4a)

Halachah states that people who work as employees are not permitted to knowingly harm themselves in a way that makes them unable to serve their employers to the best of their ability. For example, the rabbis say that one should not go to bed too late at night (Rambam, *Hilchot Sechirut* 13:5–6; *Shulchan Aruch, Choshen Mishpat* 337:19).

No one is employed so extensively as a king, who must serve his entire people. How then could King David permit himself the harm of such severe sleep deprivation? The answer is that King David had such a deep love of God in his heart that in the very act of serving God, he felt as if he was resting. His lack of sleep did not cause him any pain or harm at all. This is what King David meant when he said, "Am I not a Chasid?" This term denotes serving God out of love. "All the kings of the East and the West sleep until the third hour of the day, but I rise at midnight to give thanks to You." When all of those kings are taking a rest from serving their people, I awaken at midnight. Yet due to my deep love of God, this does not cause me to feel tired when I serve my people. (EA, *Berachot* 1, pp. 9–10)

The Inner Self Is Mysterious

One can never really know the true essence of a person. Not one's own, and certainly not that of another person. Not of an individual, definitely not of a people. We are circling around the center of knowing. We are forced to estimate and guess, to look for directions from external actions. But even these are mostly hidden from us. Indeed, just think about all the complex subconscious motivations.

And based on these little pieces of information, we try to talk about a unique personality type and soul. We must accept that our knowledge of all this rests on virtually nothing. The judgment is God's alone (Devarim 1:17). (OK 3, p. 119)

2

Torah

"Many people have left religion because in their learning... they betrayed their unique personalities."

WHEN WE SAY THAT ONE MUST DEVELOP A CONNECTION TO Torah, what exactly do we mean? Tanach, Gemara, *aggadah*, *halachah*, Jewish philosophy, and kabbalah? Yet I spent eight years in yeshiva, and the majority of time was spent on Gemara. In no way do I wish to diminish the importance of this form of learning, but there are many who connect to other parts of the Torah, yet are forced to spend their time on topics they feel least connected to. When people say that learning Torah is boring, I understand that to mean that they find a particular area of learning boring. Unfortunately, many have not been introduced to most areas of the Torah.

Say a person who had never heard music before was introduced to it for the very first time through a classical piece. Perhaps he doesn't like classical music. Would it make sense to then conclude that he does not like music? Of course not. There are so many more varieties of music that it is unlikely that he would not find something he liked if he took the time to explore more of them.

In this chapter Rav Kook encourages us to find a personal Torah – and to realize that there is not only one type of Torah, but an endless variety that can speak to countless individuals.

Studying Torah in a Personal Way

Why Some Jews Give Up Religion

This piece originally appeared in *Orot Hatorah* 9:6, edited and censored. Now that the diary entries of Rav Kook have been published in their original form, the uncensored version is available and is translated here.

Many people have left religion because in their learning and spiritual perfection, they betrayed their unique personalities. For example, a person may be naturally talented in matters of *aggadah*[1] and be unsuited to constant immersion in matters of *halachah*.[2] Yet because he does not recognize his unique talents, he occupies himself in matters of Gemara and its commentaries, since he sees that this is customary in the religious world today. But deep inside his soul he feels a hatred toward the material he is learning, since constant involvement in it does not suit his unique natural gifts.

However, if he were to find the specific type of Torah that fits his unique talents and immerse himself in it, he would then immediately recognize that the nauseating feeling he experienced when involved in matters of *halachah* was not coming from any flaw in that holy and important type of learning. It was rather his soul expressing its desire to be absorbed in another type of Torah. This person would then stay truly faithful to the Torah and become an expert in the type of Torah that is unique to him. In fact, he would even be able to help those who are more talented in *halachah* by showing them the inner peace of *aggadah*, poetry, and emotions.

Unfortunately, because this person does not recognize the true

---

1. Rav Kook is using the word *aggadah* to refer to any non-legal topic, which includes matters of philosophy, mysticism, and personal growth (i.e., musar).
2. Rav Kook is using the word *halachah* to refer to any type of learning that focuses strictly on laws and practical details. This may include the legal aspects of Mishnah and Gemara and their commentaries.

reason for his feelings of nausea toward *halachah*, he forcefully ignores his nature. And as soon as the path of a non-Torah way of life opens up to him, he breaks out and then hates and becomes an enemy of Torah and religion. He will go from one sin to another. It is from these types of people that haters of our people are created. They try to proclaim a new vision and blind the eyes of the world.

There is a great diversity of wisdom that expands even greater than this. One may be strongly attracted to a certain secular wisdom. Such a person must also follow his unique talents, while setting aside fixed times for learning Torah. If he does this, then he will succeed in both, because "Torah together with the way of the world is beautiful" (*Pirkei Avot* 2:2). And the Gemara at the end of *Yoma* discusses how to find the right balance of priorities for such people. In general, this whole issue is dependent on each person's unique soul. (KYK 1, Pinkas Acharon b'Boisk, 52)

Rav Kook's Own Struggles in Studying Torah

A man once said to Rav Kook, "My son is not motivated to study Torah." Rav Kook replied, "When I was young, I also was not excited to study *halachah*. My heart was drawn after *aggadah*. However, by studying *aggadah*, I came to study *halachah*. I suggest you teach your son *aggadah*, and as a result, he will also come to study *halachah*." (SR, p. 180)

I Know What Makes Me Unique: *Aggadah*

Inside my soul I know that my ideas concerning *halachah*, while they may be accurate explanations, do not form a new path that stands out from books already written.

On the other hand, concerning the world of *aggadah*, philosophy, and mysticism, even though I have only invested a small amount of time in them, I can see that with the help of God, I have already found a unique path. In fact, I have not come across books that contain ideas at all similar. (MS, introduction)

Rav Kook and Bialik had great respect for each other. Here, Rav Kook is talking with Bialik (standing on the right). Just as Bialik wrote a book on *aggadah*, so too did Rav Kook. On the far right is Rav Kook's own commentary on *aggadah* called *Ein Aya*.

Don't Lie to Your Soul

One should not lie to one's soul; one should not deny one's inner emotions due to the whirlwind of external approval. If one feels inspired and holy in a specific area of learning, then one must constantly satisfy oneself from this deep pleasure that one's heart desires. As for me personally, I am filled with a powerful sense of divine satisfaction when I study mystical Torah. Even if I know that this form of learning is abstract, I must be strong inside and not remove myself from it. Obviously, one must also give time to practical needs – whether concrete actions or the practical parts of Torah and wisdom. (SK 8:24)

Spiritual Books Inspire the Soul

A letter to Rabbi Tzvi Hirsch Weisfish (author of *Hafrashat Terumot u'Ma'asrot* and good friend of Rav Charlap), May 31, 1910

Your precious letter has arrived. Concerning your question: Do I have any advice that will inspire and encourage a person to serve God with joy and dedication?

The main advice I usually give to my friends and others similar to me is that one must set regular times to learn the more spiritual books of the Torah. These holy books should not be thrown off to the corner of the room and only read occasionally. When real time is invested into these spiritual books, the light of the soul will naturally shine, and there is no doubt that the spirit of joy and dedication will appear in the heart of any sincere seeker of truth. (IR 1, p. 339)

Finding One's Own Unique Spiritual Diet

There is a well-known principle that a person should not journey in the *pardes* (kabbalistic/philosophic fields) before first having filled his or her stomach with meat and wine (Tanach, Gemara, *halachah*, etc.). Perhaps this is referring to a person who only wants to fulfill the basic obligation according to the letter of the law. However, for one who feels within one's heart a strong passion to learn profound ideas, the correct principle may be as follows: "One should always learn Torah in the subject-matter that one's heart desires" (*Avodah Zarah* 19a).

The very fact that one has a special talent in philosophical or mystical subject matter is itself a proof that the will of God is for this person to be immersed in profound ideas. And furthermore, any idea that has become essential for one's quest for God – and without it, one would feel a severe lacking – becomes for such a person the meat and wine.

This is not in conflict with the principle against journeying to *pardes*, for that is only referring to matters that are beyond a person's essential needs. Therefore, one who feels a deep intellectual and emotional pull toward the understanding of God should be confident in his or her ways and sure of success. Of course, there is no question that one should set aside enough time to learn the basics of Torah and its laws in a proper way. Nevertheless, one's main learning should be in the subject matter that one's heart is most passionate about.

And if one looks around and sees that most people are not behaving in this way, one should realize that for these people it is not appropriate to enter the world of profound thoughts until they first develop in a gradual way. In addition, a person must be careful not to grow arrogant, for this is all really dependent on the natural differences between souls. We may go even further in saying that one who has the natural urge to know all these profound ideas in a clear and organized form will not be able to truly connect to God without journeying down this specific path. It can be compared to eating a diet that is wrong for one's body type. Certainly, one who does this will naturally feel weak and tired, even though another may be completely healthy on that same diet. Therefore, we must be careful not to compare one person's diet to another's.

Thus, one who is naturally drawn to profound and deep ideas should not be intimidated by others who are not. Instead, one should realize that this is one's personal obligation. Of course, it goes without saying that despite all this, basic types of learning should not be abandoned completely. Nevertheless, one must know that one will never be satisfied unless special attention is given to that which one's soul demands. Only then will one be successful in serving God with a truly deep sense of happiness. (OT 9.12)

Don't Be Intimidated by Non-Spiritual Rabbis
Even if one finds great rabbis... to whom matters of spirituality are not important... one's heart should not despair over one's inner hunger for ways of spirituality.... What difference does this make? Ultimately this is one's personal gift, and it is fitting for one to rejoice in one's unique talent. (OT 10.4)

Torah of Soul versus Torah of Law
Inspiration versus Details
IDEALISTS VERSUS REALISTS
As a rule, poets know how to describe the finer side of life, its beauty, its energy, and its flow. They also know how to describe the evils of life and to protest against them forcefully. But it is outside the abil-

ity of the idealistic imagination to uncover the particular details of how to effect change upon even the most minor defects, which can have very destructive consequences. This falls within the realm of a type of knowledge that deals with details. Here begins the work of physicians, economists, engineers, judges, and all those who pursue practical wisdom.

PROPHETS: THEIR STRENGTH AND WEAKNESS

This distinction has even wider application. The prophets saw the great evil of idolatry in ancient Israel and protested against it with all their might. They described the beauty and bliss associated with the belief in one God. They saw all the moral corruption: oppression of the poor, murder, adultery, and robbery, and they were inspired with the spirit of God to solve and prevent these conditions through lofty and holy speeches.

And yet, the little lapses from which the main body of sin developed remained hidden from the eye of every prophet and visionary. It was not within the sphere of prophecy to grasp how the regular performance of mitzvot and study of Torah would slowly release hidden inner wisdom and eventually vanquish the darkness of idolatry. Nor could it grasp how the gradually increasing carelessness [in the details], which undermines the performance of the mitzvot... would start a process of corruption... letting human passions and the straying imagination run wild...

THE UNIQUENESS OF MOSHE'S PROPHECY

It is true that this perception was granted to the prophecy of Moshe, which he received from God "from mouth to mouth" (Bamidbar 12:8). His prophecy was of undimmed clarity, understanding simultaneously the general concerns of spiritual and philosophical principles as well as the precise demands of details. But "there never arose another prophet like Moshe whom God knew face to face" (Devarim 34:10).

JUDAISM WITHOUT MOSHE RABBEINU

It was therefore necessary to assign the communication of spiritual and philosophical principles to the prophets, and the details to the rabbis. The Talmud (*Bava Batra* 12a) declares, "*Chacham adif mi'navi*" (A rabbi is better than a prophet). Prophecy, with its impassioned and fiery demands, could not accomplish healing the Jewish people of idolatry; removing the sources of oppression; and getting rid of murder, sexual perversity, and bribery. All of this was accomplished by the rabbis – through the detailed development of the Torah, by raising many *chachamim*, and by the dedicated study of each and every law and its application.

THE EXTREME FOCUS ON *HALACHAH*

In the course of time, the concern with the work of the rabbis dominated over the work of the prophets, and prophecy ceased altogether. After some time, the prominence of spiritual and philosophical principles declined; although they were implicit in the details, they were not sufficiently explained.

THE NEGATIVE REACTION OF THE MASSES

At the end of the present time period, when the light of prophecy will begin to have its revival, as we are promised, "I shall pour out My spirit on all beings" (Yoel 3:1), there will develop a noticeable disgust for the details. This is hinted to in the Talmudic statement that at the time of the messianic age, "the wisdom of the rabbis will become bitter, and those who create the limits of the law will turn from city to city without finding support" (*Sotah* 49b).

HOW TO REVIVE RESPECT FOR *HALACHAH*

This will continue until the power of prophecy will reemerge and reveal itself not as bitter, unripe fruit, but rather as fruit that is full of sweetness and life. Prophecy itself will acknowledge the great importance of the work of the rabbis, and in righteous humility exclaim: *"Chacham adif mi'navi"* (A rabbi is better than a prophet). The soul of Moshe will then reappear in the world. (O, "Zeronim" 2)

I Have a Great Desire to Synthesize
I have a great desire to connect the spiritual and practical elements of the Torah. In the ancient days, and certainly during the period of the prophets, these two elements of Torah were firmly connected. Also during the period of the Tannaim and Amoraim (sages of the Mishnah and Talmud) and within the Jerusalem Talmud, these two elements were certainly connected. The sealing of the Babylonian Talmud came to give the light of Torah the ability to illuminate the darkness; and the time has arrived to restore this movement to its peak. (SK 1:834)

Rav Kook always tried to find a way to introduce the masses to his beautiful and holistic view of Judaism. Here is Rav Kook welcoming those who came to Jerusalem for Pesach, 1929.

The Rabbanut Is Too Focused on *Halachah*
A letter to the Vaad Haklali (a general committee that dealt with the Ashkenazic community's financial and religious affairs), July 7, 1911

The Rabbanut that I am trying to raise up is a Rabbanut that is constantly involved with the day-to-day issues of the Jewish people in

Israel.... It should not be boxed in and focused only on the world of religious law... because matters of religion are in truth matters of life. (IR 2, p. 28)

Secular Jews Despise the Rabbanut
A letter to Ze'ev Gloskin (one of the founders of the Jewish colony of Rehovot), April 26, 1907

I am sending you a letter that I received from the Agudat Hacormim[3] that is located in Rechovot. This organization is full of complaints regarding the national winery. Now of course, these arguments raised need to be answered... whether to be lenient on them with a pleasant demeanor, or perhaps to clarify these matters according to the *halachah*.

Despite all of these decisions that we must make, I so desperately want to be a part of the building of the holy land of Israel together with all our brothers. Unfortunately, in the most important matters, they distance themselves from me. This is due to the general opinion of the secular Jews, who are all afraid of the influence of the Rabbanut. (IR 1, p. 80)

We Have Abandoned the Soul of the Torah
A letter to Rabbi Yehuda Leib Seltzer (Chairman of the Union of Orthodox Rabbis in America), January 4, 1913

We must not ignore the basic medicine that is capable of healing everything; it is only because we have abandoned it that our downfall has come about. It is the thing that my poor and bitter soul has become accustomed to speak about and repeat hundreds and thousands of times: "We have abandoned the soul of the Torah." This is the great cry that contains in it the power of generations upon generations: from the days of the prophets to the ancient sages, from

---

3. Association of wine growers.

the greatest rabbis of the middle ages (the Rishonim) all the way to the wisest of the current era (the Acharonim).

For too long the most talented among our people have focused almost exclusively on the practical aspects of the Torah, and even then only on specific sections of it. Yet the emotional, philosophical, and all higher spiritual wisdom – where the secrets of redemption and salvation are hidden – we have totally abandoned. In fact, if a person came and complained about this great deficiency to the leaders of the Jewish people, he would be considered arrogant and absurd. The great voices of the philosophers of God, of the most exalted Chasidim, of the purest kabbalists, who came with the secrets of God, the holy visions of courage, who waited and anticipated redemption, are like a lonely voice calling out in a desert wasteland.

For too long we have delayed dealing with this issue. Consequently, atheism has slowly arisen before us in its thick, disgraceful, dark filth. It snatches thousands of souls from our people each year. Yet despite this, in our own camp of Torah and faith, we find only darkness and no clearly defined desires and goals. We are therefore being called to return in *teshuvah* in an enormous way.... It is specifically at such a moment of crisis and danger that we need to take the greatest of all medicines. Yes, we must be radical in our approach. Any form of compromise will not solve the issue. Faith has been lost, and it is continuing to fade away because we have abandoned the Torah and there is no one to interpret and search out its secrets.

At the present moment, Orthodox Judaism is fighting a defensive and foolish war that tries to argue that the outside world is destroying itself and that all of its values and beliefs will simply be destroyed along with it. But the fact that secular Jews are more likely to fall apart than us is not an actual consolation or comfort. Truly, the suffering of the masses is not even a half consolation but rather a double agony. Pointing fingers at the sickness of our people will not bring strength and life, since this attitude is pessimistic by its very nature.

But why do we need to walk such a winding path when we could instead walk the open and straight road that stands before us? What we must do is reestablish the spiritual understanding of the entire Torah. Indeed, any person whose heart is filled with courage, whose pen is filled with strength, and whose soul is filled with the spirit of God is being called to march out into the streets and cry out loud, "Let there be light!" (IR 2, p. 123)

The Highest Form of Torah Learning

Understand the Greater Goal of Each Detail

Torah lishmah (Torah learning for its own sake, the highest form of Torah learning) is when one trains oneself to intellectually and emotionally understand how each and every detail is connected to a greater purpose, and how that great holy purpose is materialized through every detail. (OT 2.7)

Keep the Larger Vision in View

The goal of Torah learning is to internalize the main principles of the Torah, so much so that this knowledge gives power to the details of every part of *halachah*. This can be compared to the way that a healthy heart delivers blood to each limb.

Indeed, without such a clear level of knowledge, every detail seems as if it is a separate and alienated entity. This creates confusion at the very essence of the Torah and blocks a person from serving God with love and freedom. "And the word of God came to them a little here and a little there" (Yeshayahu 28:13). Words of Torah must be seen as one vision and one mitzvah. (OT 3.3)

The Demand for Holistic Spirituality

The widespread chutzpah that we are told will occur during the times of Mashiach comes about because the world has reached a stage in which people demand an understanding of how all the details of the Torah connect to a greater goal. Even one detail that is left disconnected from the greater goal causes this generation to have no rest. Now, if the world were involved in this type of Torah, so that one's soul would rise up to perceive how all the details fit into the greater goal, then *teshuvah* (spiritual growth) and *tikkun olam* (universal transformation) would come about.

Yet because of a laziness to uncover the light of the inner Torah… destruction has come into the world. Therefore, we must use the greatest medicine of all – an increase in our spiritual talents, until the understanding of how all the many ideas and actions of the Torah are connected to a greater purpose will be self-evident. Only then will the power of spiritual life – in action and knowledge – appear in the world. (SK 2:2)

Developing Clarity in *Halachah*

The amount of clarity that one has in *halachah* (Jewish law) will determine the amount of happiness one has in the performance of it. A lack of clarity and understanding causes feelings of heaviness. Some even experience an exhausting paranoia that causes a resentment of the Torah, God forbid.

In contrast, those with great clarity are not tormented by details at all. Quite the opposite – attention to detail is a sign of expertise, just as attention to grammar demonstrates the quality of one's words. (OT 9.4)

Although Rav Kook tried very hard to attach himself to the secular Zionists, he also never gave up his loving relationship to the ultra-Orthodox. In a deep sense, he spent much of his life trying to bridge the gap between two seemingly opposing worlds. Here is Rav Kook giving a speech at a ceremony for Yeshivat Chayei Olam in Jerusalem's Old City in 1926.

Finding Spiritual Meaning within *Halachah*

Sometimes, one who has the type of soul that is capable of climbing to the greatest spiritual heights will become depressed and saddened when immersed in the little details of *halachah*. Such a person may feel imprisoned, almost as if chained inside the law. Nevertheless, the solution is not to abandon *halachah*. Rather, one must train oneself to seek the value of every detail until one finds its spiritual source and significance. (OT 9.8)

Poetry in Laws

Just as there are laws in poetry, there is poetry in laws. (*Otzrot Hare'iyah* 2, p. 393)

3
God

"There is a type of atheism that is really faith."

MANY PEOPLE THINK THAT ATHEISTS ARE THE GREAT ENEMY OF religion. They try to destroy faith in God by using scientific arguments, or by mocking the very notion of a "Great Being" watching over us. While in the past, a person who denied the existence of God would be excommunicated from society, today, a person who proudly acknowledges belief in God can feel like the alienated one. Some religious people avoid discussing God with atheists; others try to argue. Yet when a person reads the writings of Rav Kook, one finds a very different approach to atheism.

Not only does Rav Kook not try to avoid or argue with the atheist, he actually legitimizes and even praises the atheists' denial. When Rav Kook would read a book refuting the existence of an egocentric God in heaven who demands praises and subjugation, he felt no need to argue back. In fact, he agreed with the criticism. Rav Kook believed that many atheists who think they are denying God are in fact only denying an immature and distorted image of God. In other words, this person's denial of God is really a deeper quest for a higher, more sophisticated understanding.

In this chapter, Rav Kook will explain what he thinks atheists have to teach religious people, and what we really mean when we say the word *God*.

The Need to Mature One's Understanding of God

What Do We Mean When We Say "God"?

GOD IS BEYOND OUR GRASP

All disagreements between people and all inner conflicts that one suffers in one's own mind are only the result of confusion concerning the concept of God. God is an endless ocean that is both the source and destination of all practical and theoretical thoughts.[1]

We must constantly purify our thoughts concerning God so that they will be clean of any false beliefs, absurd fears, negative characteristics, or major gaps in comprehension. Belief in God will only bring happiness to a person to the degree that the greatness of God is investigated and understood. When this work is begun, the soul starts to shine from a higher source.

The essence of faith is the belief in the greatness and perfection of the Infinite One, the belief that anything that enters the heart about such matters is merely a tiny spark compared to what one should have imagined. And that which one should have imagined does not even come close to that which is actually true. When one speaks of goodness, kindness, justice, power, or beauty, about anything that is life or the enhancement of life, about faith and spirituality – it is all the desire of the soul to express that which is beyond all things. All the names and descriptions, whether in Hebrew or another lan-

---

1. My teacher, Rabbi David Aaron, was the first person to introduce me to these writings about Rav Kook's understanding of God. Rabbi David Aaron has written extensively about Rav Kook's belief that all misconceptions of religion come down to our simplistic and immature understanding of God. See his works *Endless Light, The Ancient Path of the Kabbalah to Love, Spiritual Growth, and Personal Power* (New York: Simon and Schuster, 1997), *Seeing God: Ten Life-Changing Lessons of the Kabbalah* (New York: Jeremy P Tarcher/Putnam, 2001), and *The Secret Life of God: Discovering the Divine within You* (Boston: Shambhala, 2004).

guage, only express a small and dim spark of the hidden light that the souls yearns for when it proclaims "God."

THE WORD *GOD* IS INADEQUATE

Any limit one puts on God brings one to atheism. The very concept of describing God is spiritual idol worship. Even the limits of "intelligence" or "will" or "spirituality," even the word *Elohim* (God) itself, when not understood to be mere sparks of that which is beyond these descriptions, would also bring one to atheism.

Any description besides Ein Sof (Infinite) is only there to help bring one to the source of faith. Some descriptions may be classified as "limbs of the King," while other descriptions may be called "clothes of the King." While it is true that one who mocks the clothes of the king has committed a serious offense and may forfeit his life, one must still be aware of the distinction between the essence of faith and descriptions of faith, and even between the different levels of descriptions of faith.

IMMATURE FAITH TRIES TO CRYSTALIZE GOD

The greatest impairment for the spirit of humankind is when the idea of God becomes crystalized in a specific way due to habit and childish imagination. This is a form of the sin of creating an idol that we must stay away from.

Due to the general lack of learning about these matters, the concept of God becomes obscure.... Since even the clearest understanding of God is blurry, the concept of God that prevails among the masses – and even among the individuals who are supposed to be their leaders – is that of a powerful tyrant whom no one can escape and all are forced to worship. When a person comes to serve God with this skewed belief, full of darkness and chaos and lacking any intelligence or Torah understanding, one begins to lose one's spiritual light. No greatness of God is then manifest in one's soul. There are only wild imaginings of a false concept of reality that terrify anyone who believes in them. This crushes one's spirit, perverts the emotions, and dulls one's spiritual sensitivity. It uproots the godly spark within one's soul. Such a person may proclaim all day long the belief in God and His Oneness, but these are empty words that the soul has nothing to do with.

ATHEISM IS A CURE FOR IMMATURE FAITH

The tendency of simplistic people to understand the reality of God based on words and letters alone is a source of embarrassment for humankind. Atheism comes like a painful cry to redeem mankind from this narrow, alien pit, and to raise it up from the darkness of text and speech to the light of thoughts and emotions, and eventually, to place its main focus on morality. Therefore, atheism has a temporary function and worth. It comes to purify the dirt that has stuck to a faith that lacks any comprehension.

A person who recognizes the good within atheism and tastes its sweetness can draw it back to its holy source.... The ideology that wants to abandon the tradition of our forefathers due to its new vision is in truth an ideology of *teshuvah*. When a person understands the profound criticism of faith that atheism offers, one is able to transform its destructive force into a drive for return to the true God. (O, "Zeronim" 5)

Secular Zionists in Israel, being accustomed to the religious Jews of the Old Yishuv (whom they believed shunned secular education and avoided contact with any society outside their own), were amazed by Rav Kook. Here was a man who looked like the religious Jews in Jerusalem, yet spoke with worldly sophistication, had an incredible breadth of knowledge in many secular subjects, and approached them with appreciation and respect. This is a picture of Rav Kook in his old age.

"I Love God"
I am full of love for God. I know that what I seek, what I love, cannot be called by a name. How can one give a name to that which is greater than everything, greater than good, greater than essence, greater than existence?! Yet I love, and I say, "I love God." (SK 1:164)

Atheists Who Have a Deep Faith
There is a type of atheism that is really faith, and a type of faith that is really atheism. How so? One may acknowledge that the Torah is from heaven, yet have an image of heaven so immature that it does not have even a trace of true faith.

What is an atheism that is really like faith? One may deny that the Torah is from heaven, yet such a denial is based on a concept of heaven that was received from minds filled with incorrect beliefs. The atheist says that the Torah must have some other source and begins to search for meaning through the moral and intellectual spirit of mankind. Even though this person may not have arrived at ultimate understanding, this type of atheism is a kind of faith that in time will bring one closer and closer to a more complete truth.

This is an upside-down generation that needs much help. The debate of whether or not Torah is from heaven is a good example by which to explain many debates in faith. For what we are truly dealing with is the difference between what people say simply with their mouths and what they actually mean inside. The latter is what really matters. (OE, p. 25)

Religious People Who Are Miserable
Honoring God can lead to either empowerment or weakness. Giving honor to God should give birth to an inner courage within man.... But there are people who in their fear and anxiety do not dare to contemplate and investigate the concept of God, and so their image of God becomes a stumbling block. Serving God is then the fulfill-

ment of a selfish demand from a Being that desires endless honor. This belief corrupts all sensitive and pure emotions and depresses people, transforming them into base slaves who hate each other. In truth, it is God whom they hate in their hearts, even though they speak words of love and honor toward Him. "In their mouths and their lips they honor Him; nevertheless, their hearts are far from Him" (Yeshayahu 29:13). (MiR, "Kavod" 3)

Believers Can Crush Faith; Atheists Can Inspire It
A person can sometimes be damaged by books written by those of small faith, those whose souls are not filled with the powerful holiness of spiritual fire. On the other hand, books written by total atheists who are filled with the powerful but impure spirit of denial can inspire and cure the weary soul, filling one with life and energy, with spiritual strength and passionate faith in God. (OE, p. 21)

Atheists with More Faith Than Religious People
Sometimes one finds an atheist who has a powerful inner faith that shines from the source of spiritual holiness, much greater than the weaker faith of thousands of believers. This principle is true regarding individuals as well as generations. (OE, p. 21)

Arguing over Language
When it comes to matters of philosophy and belief, whose content is abstract and spiritual, it often happens that people have a disagreement only externally, while on a deeper level they are referring to the same thing. Their entire disagreement, which seems so intense, is simply an argument over language. Each side does not understand the words the other is using. (SK 1:10)

The Language of Faith Is Not the Ultimate Goal
All the specific words in books that discuss faith are nothing but ways of explanation. And while it is helpful to use this language to

describe the inner essence of that which is beyond all thoughts and words, it should never be the ultimate goal. Therefore, we sometimes find people who do not have any connection to the words of faith, yet are nonetheless filled with its inner essence. Such people are often not aware of their spiritual greatness; they are the people who despite having lost their belief are full of many powerful moral actions. (KYK 2, Pinkas 4:86)

Any Name of God Is Too Limited for Our Souls
When we come to speak about God from the depths of our souls, any name that we use is too limited. We say the names, and we realize that their inner light is being suffocated by those expressions. It is through this spiritual pain that our soul expands. "From the depths, I called out to God, who answered me with divine expansion" (Tehillim 118:5). (SK 1:883)

Do Not Let Language Intimidate You
We should not be intimidated if after a long period of the Jewish people's influence upon itself and the world, atheism returns and spreads. "If so, 'What has the righteous one done?'" (Tehillim 11:3). *Tikkun olam* (universal transformation) is not recognizable through the type of words people use. The main point is the inner transformation of the individual soul and the greater world.... Within is the light of God and wisdom of God, even when it is veiled in the clothing of atheism. (SK 1:377)

Each Person Has a Unique Understanding of God
The variety of ways of understanding God all have elements of truth; each soul is drawn to a different understanding. No person can truly understand another person's inner attitude toward God. All external comparisons of common words or similar lifestyles are superficial; each person's inner attitude is always different and unique. (SK 1:23)

How Does One Experience God?

God Doesn't Exist, He Is Existence

COUNTERFEIT MEANING

It is impossible for the soul to have a firm foundation in anything but God. All of one's knowledge, emotions, imagination, internal and external desires, and movements need to be directed toward God. Only then will one find fulfillment, harmony, and peace of mind.

However, if one asks for anything less than this greatness, one will be overwhelmed like a sinking ship amidst roaring waves, tossed from one to the next until one no longer knows who one is. If a person does succeed in dwelling in some thick mud of fake spirit and materialistic emotion, one's light may be diminished for a short time so that one can convince oneself of having found fulfillment. However, it will not be long until one's spirit breaks out of its chains and begins to protest in full force. Indeed, only in God can we find fulfillment.

LOOKING FOR GOD IN THE WRONG PLACE

But is not God outside of the reality of our emotions and thoughts? And anything that is beyond emotion and thought, from our point of view, is nothing. How can we find peace of mind in nothing?

As a consequence, we find many *talmidei chachamim* (religious experts) who seek God but feel exhaustion in their souls. For when their souls yearn for the brightest light, they are not satisfied with the type of light found in morality, truth, or beauty, even in their highest forms. The world becomes meaningless in their eyes. The yearning of their souls grows so much that the entire world, both physical and spiritual, seems too constricted to them: its very atmosphere begins to choke them.

They are searching for that which is above their limits, that which feels like nothing. But it is impossible to transform nothing into something, and thus their overall desire for life and the pursuit of God becomes tired and weak.

IMMANENT CONNECTION TO GOD
What is the path that leads to the palace? It is the Godliness that is manifest in the world in its beauty and glory, spirit and soul; in all animals and bugs, bushes and flowers; in all nations and states, oceans and waves; in the skies and the magnificent stars; in the style of great speakers, the ideas of authors, the imagination of singers, the thoughts of scholars, the emotions of sensitive people, and in the courage of every warrior.

TRANSCENDENT CONNECTION TO GOD
The yearning to encounter the transcendent God, to be swallowed up inside Him and to be gathered into His light, is a desire that we are unable to satisfy. Yet there are moments when the transcendent descends to the world for us and we encounter an unearthly pleasure and peace of mind. We are struck by lightning from a realm that is above all thought and theory. The heavens open up and we see the vision of God.

Nevertheless, we know that this state of consciousness is only momentary. The lightning disappears, and we return to dwell not inside the palace but rather in the courtyards of God. (O, "Zeronim" 1)

"Religion" Is Not a Jewish Concept
The belief that God is only relevant within religion has caused us to perceive the world in an extremely empty way. God must be evident within all of life and existence; and as a consequence, God will be experienced within all of life and existence. Religion is simply a way to train one's actions, personality, and feelings... so that life and all of existence will be an experience of God.

God is only found in religion when religion becomes something that is greater than itself. Religion is a fine name for other nations, but not so for the Jewish people. The life of Torah is not simply religion. Our life of Torah is the revelation of God that comes from all of existence. Torah and existence, when they are united, reveal God in life and within the individual and collective soul. Yet from the perspective of ordinary religion, the holy and the secular are separate. Such a religion desires to control matters of the holy and abandon matters of the secular. Yet God is revealed in everything, inside both the holy and the secular. (KYK 2, Pinkas 1:20)

Monotheism versus Panentheism

MONOTHEISM CAN WEAKEN YOU

The regular understanding of God that comes from monotheism, which is the most popular understanding of faith, will sometimes cause sadness and anxiety. This feeling of weakness is caused when man perceives himself as an object that is manipulated, limited, fragile, and distant from the perfection of God, Who shines in the light of beauty and power. In particular, the feeling of weakness is aroused when one compares the obvious moral weaknesses of man to the righteous and ethical perfection of God. While it is possible to decrease this feeling of weakness by strengthening one's moral standards, the feeling will never completely go away due to man's inability in his inescapable smallness to compare to the greatness of an Infinite God.

PANENTHEISM EMPOWERS YOU

The monotheistic understanding of God that tends toward pantheism[2] can prevent such feelings of weakness. When this perspective

---

2. Rav Kook uses two terms here: monotheism and pantheism. Monotheism literally means "one God." It is the belief that there is one God who created the universe; God, however, is not the universe. Pantheism literally means "everything is God." It is the belief that God is the same as the universe. When Rav Kook says "a monotheistic understanding of God that tends toward pantheism," he means a third option, which is today called panentheism (Rav Kook may not have been familiar with this specific term). Panentheism literally means "all in

is purified of its possible distortions, it resembles the new Chasidic understanding that there is nothing besides God.

If this perspective is not understood correctly, there is still a danger of feeling absolute weakness and nothingness. In fact, one can feel even more intense nothingness than the nothingness of pure monotheism; at least in a simple monotheistic perspective one existed in one's own reality, albeit feeling small and insignificant compared to the great perfection of God. However, when it is vaguely understood that there is nothing in the world except for God, one can feel that one's own consciousness is not merely insignificant, but entirely false and illusionary. Consequently, this second perspective can potentially weaken one's spirit even more than the first.

However, this is not the real truth. The second perspective should actually fill a person with strength and confidence. It encourages one to distance oneself from the ways of life that are caused by the false idea that people are separate entities in and of themselves, spiritually cut off from God. Once one begins to walk on this true path, one no longer has to conquer anything in concrete reality. Endless happiness will be found merely by conquering false beliefs. To be sure, this spiritual work is not as simple as it sounds. To free oneself from the chains of false beliefs is often not any easier than freeing oneself from physical chains. Yet a spirit of empowerment is waiting at the end of the road of the second perspective.

THE NEED TO COMBINE THE TWO PERSPECTIVES
However, it is only possible to reach the second state of consciousness through great physical and intellectual training in the first perspective. Then one can shine the light of the second perspective into the first. "God in His holy sanctuary" (Tehillim 11:4). The

---

God." It is the belief that although God's presence fills the universe, God also transcends the universe.

second perspective allows the world to be experienced with more intellectual and emotional truth, filled with the light of humility. Nevertheless, the physical world cannot function practically with only this higher perspective. Thus, one must diminish one's light in order to adapt to the concrete world and stay firmly connected to the first perspective, while at the same time being absolutely clear that this perspective on its own is not the real truth. The first perspective needs to be guided by the second, more profound perspective.

When this combination occurs, the physical world functions well, precisely and justly, while the inner world of thought remains clear and becomes elevated. Then the world can exist in harmony and perfect unity (OK 3, pp. 399–401)

4
The Meaning of Life

"When one realizes that being totally perfect is unattainable, one can finally understand that one's true greatness is found in the holy journey of constantly becoming just a little bit better."

WHEN ONE STUDIES THE RELIGIONS OF THE EAST (BUDDHISM OR Hinduism, for example), one often finds charts and maps describing a path to spiritual enlightenment. By following the directions and advice set down, one intends to achieve the end goal that is described and pictured in much detail.

In contrast, a person who decides to go to a class on Judaism will often hear a nice *dvar Torah* about the importance of Shabbat, or another one about the importance of Torah study, or still another one about the importance of *teshuvah* or *kashrut*. While all of this is fine, eventually one may get the feeling that Judaism, while possessing many beautiful ideas, has no particular destination to which all of these ideas are leading one.

Does Judaism have an ultimate goal that all of the mitzvot point to? Is there an all-encompassing objective that all of the seemingly random concepts and laws are trying to help us achieve?

In this chapter, Rav Kook describes the purpose he believes Judaism is trying to help us actualize.

Is Perfection the Goal?

Jealousy of God's Perfection

REPRESSED JEALOUSY

There is a hidden inclination within the depths of the soul that rots the bones and brings weakness and darkness to any thought of light. This jealousy is mysterious. Indeed, many will not recognize it due to the many causes that prevent the mouth from articulating it. Nevertheless, it is there, resting in the human subconscious. This jealousy will sometimes express itself in various ways outside of its true form, just as any jealousy may clothe itself under a foreign name.

WE ARE JEALOUS OF GOD'S PERFECTION

This mysterious jealousy is the jealousy of God. Humans are jealous of God's endless happiness and perfection. This jealousy causes knowledge to be twisted, the mind to be darkened, the intellect to be distorted, and the spirit to be angered. And when all efforts are unsuccessful in containing this rage, a person is driven to absolute denial of God. This is a way of removing from the suffering soul the venom of jealousy that pierces so deep. There is no solution for this jealousy other than a clearer, more enlightened understanding of God.

CURING THE SICKNESS

When the sickness of jealousy is removed, all its negative consequences, including the empty atheism that our generation is crippled with, will be removed. The specific path to removing this sickness can be broken up into two main parts: intellectual purification and ethical enlightenment.

FIRST PATH: INTELLECTUAL PURIFICATION

The path of intellectual purification explains that the distinction between God and the world is entirely dependent on one's knowledge, perception, and way of life. The more one's perception is elevated, the closer humans and the world come to the greatness of God. When one's perception reaches its peak, one begins to understand that all is actually within God, and all the details of the universe are mere manifestations of the Divine, expressed in different forms in front of our eyes. Consequently, God's happiness is in truth everyone's happiness.

This happiness continues to spread to the extent that one's knowledge of God is clarified. This is the great secret pleasure that comes from understanding God. A person begins to sense the divine happiness, perfection that is full of joy and power. There is no longer any room for jealousy.

SECOND PATH: ETHICAL ENLIGHTENMENT

The second path is of ethical enlightenment, which explains that godly perfection is dependent on the attribute of freely chosen righteousness. Those who choose to uplift the freedom of their will to the same attribute of righteousness, which is God's greatest trait, are actually drawing from "the body of the King" (a well-known kabbalistic phrase). Because they have become humble in the light of God, it can be said that they have achieved godly perfection.

Indeed, there is nothing preventing us from elevating our free will to godly righteousness. And the more one is able to grow toward this, the more one has transformed into a godly human. Godly perfection belongs to God by virtue of His freedom to choose righteousness, and this is an ability to which all people also have access. Therefore there is no room for jealousy. (OK 2, pp. 397–98)

The Spiritual Importance of Growth

Two Types of Perfection

From our perspective, we understand two categories of absolute godly perfection.[1] One type of perfection may be explained as

---

1. My teacher, Rabbi David Aaron, has written an important book explaining Rav Kook's belief that God has two types of perfections. See *The Secret Life of God*.

thorough and complete, with no possibility of additional growth. However, the absence of potential for growth is itself an imperfection. Certainly, progress and development possess certain benefits and advantages to which we aspire. It cannot be possible that godly perfection would be lacking this value of growth.

We must therefore conclude that God also has the ability to grow and become actualized in infinite measure. It is the soul of God that energizes the world via its never-ending growth and self-actualization. (OK 2, p. 532)

God Needs Human Growth

From that which has been revealed to us, we know that God's secret purpose for the universe is eternal growth and development. If there were no world of imperfection, then there would be only greatness and fullness with no possibility for constant growth and increased blessing.

While it is true that there is an infinite perfection that has no possibility for growth (God Himself), within this perfection is included the magnificent power of constant growth (the physical world). Absolute, static perfection is actually enhanced by the perfection of improving from small to great. God needs the potential of this work of growth to complete Him. (OK 2, p. 530)

Journey People and Destination People

"A person should not take rushed steps" (*Berachot* 43b). There is a debate among people concerning how important a journey is in relation to its goal. For some individuals, there is a great divide between the goal and the journey. Having decided on a certain goal, one feels as if the entire detailed journey is some heavy burden. One feels frustrated and tries to rush and hurry everything. Deep inside one's soul, one feels discomfort and pain. For example, one who dreams of becoming very wealthy may set a specific amount of money as a goal and concentrate all of his or her willpower on reaching it. However, each step on the way to this goal leaves such a person unsatisfied and frustrated.

Such a goal-oriented mental state begins to affect one's physical movements, until one starts taking rushed steps. All of one's steps are simply an effort to remove the frustrating requirement of the journey.

A wise person understands that each and every step has the profound effect of bringing one to a greater level of perfection. This person knows that the very journey of reaching perfection should be valued and treasured. One who thinks this way will find a constant satisfaction and peace of mind in each and every step. This is the meaning of "in all of your ways, know Him" (Mishlei 3:6). A consequence of this state of mind is that even one's physical movements become relaxed and unrushed.

When one realizes that being totally perfect is unattainable, one can finally understand that one's true greatness is found in the holy journey of constantly becoming just a little bit better. (EA, *Berachot* 2, p. 33)

Experiencing God in the Present Moment

"In all of your ways, know Him" (Mishlei 3:6). One must search for God in everything one does. When praying, one must search for God by trying to focus on the words of prayer with deep concentration and a dedicated heart. One must not search for God in other matters at that moment. Indeed, while involved in that specific action, it may be said that God can be found within that action and nothing else. When studying Torah, one must realize that God is found in the very act of analyzing and trying to understand each idea. At that moment, God reveals Himself in that specific action and not in anything else. And finally, when involved in *gemilut chasadim* (acts of kindness), one must search for God by trying to uncover the best possible way to help one's friend.

This principle is true in all actions that a person does. Do not all matters in the world uncover the Divine? Therefore, everything a person does should be understood as a mitzvah, because one must search for God in every action. We may accurately say that one who dedicates his or her entire mind and strength to performing every action with the greatest level of perfection knows God in all of his ways. (MA 2.2)

Every Act of Growth Changes the World
A letter to Rabbi Tzvi Hirsch Weisfish (author of *Hafrashat Terumot u'Ma'asrot* and good friend of Rav Charlap), May 31, 1910

Do I have any advice that will inspire and encourage a person to serve God with joy and dedication?

... The truth is that it is extremely difficult to explain in a few words even just one of the principles of authentic spiritual work.... And yet, having said this, I will not hold back from explaining to you a great spiritual lesson. Of course, even this idea will not be truly understood until it is reviewed and studied in much greater depth. But it can still be of some help in motivating a person toward a greater love of God and the holy Torah.

It is only logical that if you could convince even the lowliest people that they were capable of doing acts of kindness that can benefit the entire world... they would be inspired to do these actions of kindness with joy and dedication. In a profound way, all laziness and fatigue that a person experiences is rooted in one's lack of belief that through one's own actions of learning Torah, doing mitzvot, praying, and improving oneself, one is actually transforming the entire universe for the better.

This is why God enlightened our eyes with the holy words of the true kabbalistic masters. These wise men have explained to us how tremendously important all of our actions are in transforming the entire universe. (IR 1, p. 339)

5

Teshuvah and Personal Growth

"The way to truly heal an individual is by uncovering the wellspring of strength and health that is hidden within the self."

AS YOM KIPPUR COMES AROUND EACH YEAR, AN ATMOSPHERE OF anxiety, fear, and guilt comes along with it. How many times have I sinned against God? Why do I lose my patience so much? Am I a bad person? Why am I so imperfect?

On the other hand, why should I say sorry to God? Is it not God who gave me a *yetzer hara* (negative impulses)? I didn't choose my personality. Must I really apologize for being myself? It is all very confusing.

Rav Kook was deeply bothered by these problems. This is the topic he confronts in this chapter.

All of One's Passions Are Inherently Good

To Trust One's Feelings

One must believe in oneself; one must believe that one's life and feelings come directly from the essence of one's soul, are good, and lead one upon a straight path.

The Torah must be a lamp to one's feet, by means of which one will see where error is likely – for at times the spirit will go astray upon a pathless wasteland. But the constant attitude must be one of spiritual confidence.

A Jew is obligated to believe that a divine soul, in essence one letter of the Torah, dwells within him. And a letter of the Torah is a complete world, constantly and infinitely growing. The wisdom within a grain of sand cannot be measured; all the years of our lives would not be sufficient to explain the entire wealth of wisdom that lies within it. How much more must we believe clearly and enthusiastically in the depth and wisdom of the entire Jewish people, its life and intuitions, and proceed confidently. Only then will we know how to use the light of the living Torah. (OTs 11:2)

The Healthy Unconscious Is the Real You

The way to truly heal an individual is by uncovering the wellspring of strength and health that is hidden within the self. It is through the revealing of the soul within the soul, the uncovering of the unconscious self that is so hidden and covered up that often people do not even recognize their own essence.

It is obvious that spiritual sicknesses and their physical manifestations come directly from the unclean parts of the self. This polluted area is the conscious self, the external and surface identity of a person.

But the hidden self, the unconscious self, has endless courage, life, and strength. In truth, from the storehouse of one's inner health, a person has enough power to influence the conscious and surface level of the self. It reminds the misleading voice that accuses oneself of being sick and broken that in reality, one's essence is brave, healthy, and full of life and strength. (MaR, p. 156)

The Holy Motivation behind All Actions
Not only in neutral matters, but also in every mistake and sin, in every failure, in every incorrect belief, there exists some spark of goodness and holy ideal that is sustaining and energizing the soul. (SK 2:350)

How Do You Know If a Desire Is Godly?
If a desire is sourced in the root of one's soul, it will eventually come to expression and will be lasting. When a desire does not have its source in the true nature of one's soul, but rather in some passing illusion, it will ultimately disappear. (EA, *Shabbat* 1, p. 146)

The Fake Self and the True Self
Only holiness, individual and universal, has its own character and its own source of life. But the non-holy, and all the more so the evil and impure, do not have their own personality or their own essential desires. They are only being propelled by external means, which move one to physical or spiritual actions. The source of desire, passion, and personality is in the realm of the holy, and those who are connected to it will be affected by it. (SK 5:39)

Unhealthy Ways People Seek Meaning
Many deficient morals and bad actions are actually motivated by a great desire hidden within the soul of humanity to taste the light of wisdom and truth – the light of God. Yet when people do not find a path that satisfies this inner thirst, they are filled with sickness and anger. In fact, they are often so confused that they try to quench their thirst with things that do not satisfy, but only serve to distract their emotions so that they do not feel the pain within their hearts. For-

tunate is the person who carries this heavy load toward the spiritual work of seeking God and quenches his or her thirst with the source of living water, the God of truth. (KYK 1, Pinkas Rishon l'Yaffo 8)

The Danger of *Teshuvah*

People often mistakenly believe that anything one does must be a part of one's essential personality. This is the work of the *yetzer hara*. This often happens after a person has done a *cheshbon hanefesh* (self-reflection; literally, "an accounting of the soul") and has a sincere thirst of the soul to align its ways with God. Now, in seeing how far one has distanced oneself from the path of holiness, one begins to feel weakened and embarrassed, depressed and fatigued.

Those who come to serve God but have not first learned how to do so will err in this performance. They will think that feelings of weakness and depression are the essential component of *cheshbon hanefesh*. However, the soul will not readily accept that which contradicts its essence. And thus, it will be burdened with sadness and will not grow in action and wisdom. Concerning this it is said, "The effort of fools exhausts them; they do not know how to get to the city" (Kohelet 10:15). Therefore, it is important to learn and investigate the nature of personal growth according to the depths of our Sages' words, as well as with the logical minds that God gave us. (MA 4.1)

The Purpose of Spiritual Growth

The purpose of all personal growth is to put each and every power, potential, and talent in its correct place and not to confuse their natural order, thereby preventing their expression. God made both people and the world inherently good, providing them with all of the tools necessary to improve the body and the soul. Anyone who perverts the divine order can only cause damage and destruction.

This can be compared to one who suppresses one's body from its natural movement. For example, if one always lay in bed, never moving from one's position and never stretching one's limbs, one would naturally damage one's body. So too, one who holds back one's soul from its natural movements is suppressing its essence and causing its destruction. (MA 2.3)

The Spiritual Importance of Growing Slowly

Sudden versus Gradual *Teshuvah*
Concerning the amount of time it takes, *teshuvah* can be broken up into two categories: sudden *teshuvah* and gradual *teshuvah*.

Sudden *teshuvah* comes from a flash of inspiration that enters the soul. One recognizes the bad and the damage of one's sins and becomes transformed into a new person.

On the other hand, gradual *teshuvah* is not like the flash of lighting that transforms the depths of bad to good. Instead, one senses that one must generally grow and steadily improve one's actions, desires, and thoughts. Little by little, one will attain the path of righteousness. (OTs 2)

The Danger of Wanting to Be a Perfect *Tzaddik*
When one is set on becoming a perfect *tzaddik* (righteous person), it is hard for one to be a *baal teshuvah* (a person of growth). Therefore, one should rather set one's heart on being a *baal teshuvah*, one who is immersed in thoughts and actions of improvement. Only then can *teshuvah* raise one up. (OTs 14:36)

The Danger of Skipping Levels of Growth
In every stage of growth there is a treasure of holiness. When one tries to skip levels, one loses out on the holy wisdom of the earlier stages. One will thus not really comprehend the higher level one skipped to because of this deficiency in one's knowledge and understanding.

One must then do *teshuvah* and return with both a broken heart and joy to the levels of growth that were skipped. Nevertheless, one should never forget the inspiration gained in the higher levels. Indeed, once a person ascends, he never really descends. Eventually the entire experience will be transformed for the good. (SK 6:253)

Teshuvah Is a Never-Ending Journey

The call to purify one's character never ends. One may have already purified it when on an intermediate spiritual level; however, after growing further, new mysteries of life that have never yet been exposed emerge from the depths of chaos for one to refine and clarify.

There are holy people who never cease growing. They go *me'chayil el chayil* (from strength to strength), always engaged in practical repentance, of which purifying and refining one's character is a vital ingredient. (OK 3, p. 233)

Focus on What You Can Fix

Whatever one is able to fix, one should focus on and not neglect to correct it. However, what one is unable to fix, one should not focus on constantly, fulfilling the verse, "The worry in one's heart should be cast out" (Mishlei 12:25). One should be involved in transforming one's soul and the world at large to the best of one's ability, and through this one will bring about the fulfillment of the verse "Commit to God in your actions, and He will establish your plans" (Mishlei 16:3). (SK 3:360)

How Idealism Can Undermine Growth

When a person tries to attain the highest levels of piety, the *yetzer hara* is strengthened. One's spirituality then often begins to diminish and become exhausted because a person reacts by using up most of one's energy to fight with the *yetzer hara*, while one could have used that energy for ascending to higher levels of growth. Therefore, a person need not seek out immediate ascent to the highest spiritual levels, but rather can be passionate about growing little by little.

Yet at the same time, one's face should always be directed toward the highest of heights. In fact, people are obligated to ask themselves, "When will my actions reach the actions of my forefathers, Avraham, Yitzchak, and Yaakov?" (*Tanna d'Bei Eliyahu* 25). And through the small strengthening of the *yetzer hara* that comes through this more general aspiration, one will awaken within oneself holy courage, and the light of life will shine from inside. (OK 3, p. 258)

Rest for the Sake of Work

There are times when a person must learn to relax the mind and not be worried by the obligations of mitzvot and learning. One must give oneself some rest in order that one's soul will grow at its own pace and travel on its own inner journey. And only after this type of "Shabbat" rest will the soul find strength to resume its growth with an even greater energy. All of the detailed mitzvot will then be fulfilled with freshness, drawing energy from the source of life. (OK 3, p. 258)

The Art of Relaxation

There is a type of commitment to work that destroys all of one's spiritual powers. On the other hand, there is a type of relaxation that fills the inner world of a person with holiness and strength. This is the secret of silence. (SK 1:445)

Specific *Teshuvah* versus General *Teshuvah*

There is a type of *teshuvah* that is focused on a specific mistake. One thinks about a certain fault and is pained by it. The soul struggles until it can eventually rise up and be liberated from the chains of this sin.

Then there is another type of *teshuvah* that is general and unspecified. No particular mistakes of the past take hold of one's mind and heart; rather, one feels a general sense of sadness and the burden of countless mistakes. One feels as if God's light does not shine upon one's life, and one lacks inner confidence. The heart is numb, the mind slow, and one is ashamed of oneself. With this embittered emotion, *teshuvah* begins. The knowledge that *teshuvah* can heal oneself brings a feeling of relief. One begins, in a broad and general way, to become a better person. (OTs 3)

The Need to Distinguish between Good and Bad

When doing *teshuvah*, one must carefully clarify the essence of good and the essence of bad in order that regret and upheaval will be directed only toward the bad and not the good. And with the very same power with which one must distance oneself from evil, one must take the good that exists within that evil and encourage it. Consequently, *teshuvah* will be a positive power that completely transforms all sins to merits. (OTs 9:5)

Holy Guilt: Sadness That Encourages

Awareness of Mistakes Signals Growth

When one makes the decision to do *teshuvah*, to improve one's actions, emotions, or even one's thoughts, one should not fall into despair due to a new awareness of one's mistakes. As long as one is surrounded by negative character traits, one is naturally not entirely conscious of one's flaws. Indeed, sometimes one is not conscious of them at all, and one may even perceive oneself as being a *tzaddik*.

However, once the voice of morality has been awakened, one's soul becomes more conscious of itself and is aware of all of its faults. One can begin to experience a great anxiety due to this lack of perfection. One must realize that this new consciousness and anxiety are the clearest signs that one is on the path of growth. Therefore, this guilt should be a source of encouragement. (OTs 8:16)

Sadness That Inspires Self-Improvement

The despair that enters one's heart is a sign of the pangs of one's conscience. It comes from a deep desire for self-improvement and holiness. Therefore, the very sadness itself should be reassuring. One should not fear it; instead, one should confront one's mistakes with both courage and tranquility. (OTs 8:15)

A Broken Spirit Proves You've Grown

Sometimes one can become depressed and allow bitterness over one's mistakes and the decline of one's personal moral standards to prevent one from even lifting one's head to study Torah or perform mitzvot, let alone to do these things with any type of joy or fulfillment.

One must realize that this very feeling of a broken spirit is a proof that one is at this moment a *baal teshuvah gamur* (a person of outstanding growth). If so, one has already reached a new level of growth. Thus, one can have peace of mind and return to a state of happiness, immersing oneself in good deeds with a content heart. (OTs 14:23)

Looking at One's Mistakes with Joy

One must understand the profound nature of *teshuvah*. *Teshuvah* should shine so powerfully that remembering a sin actually awakens a feeling of profound joy. Joy comes from the knowledge that by doing *teshuvah*, one gives value and purpose to one's past mistakes. (OTs 7:7)

To Reinterpret One's Sins

When one does *teshuvah b'ahavah* (with love for God) from one's innermost being, one begins to understand how everything that one did in the past was truly good and beneficial. When one tries to transform one's sins into merits, one does not create them anew, but instead recovers and reinterprets their essence. (SK 5:9)

The Need to Forgive Oneself

When one does *teshuvah b'ahavah* from one's innermost being, one needs to forgive oneself for all of one's sins and mistakes, just as one would want forgiveness from a friend one has wronged. Once one can see oneself as a person who is forgiven for all sins, God will transform all those sins into merits. (SK 1:671)

6

Character Traits

> *"As long as a person has not developed the ability to distinguish between the true definition of a character trait and a false one, spiritual transformation will not come about."*

MANY *MUSAR SEFARIM* (JEWISH SELF-HELP BOOKS) FOCUS THEIR readers' attention on positive *middot* (character traits) that they should seek to embody, and negative ones that they should avoid. Good character traits often include humility, patience, modesty, fear of God, and happiness, while negative character traits may include arrogance, anger, and depression. The goal is to explain what is good and what is bad, so that one will know how to behave correctly.

Yet Rav Kook believed that something was missing in this approach. He worried that people would come to damage themselves and others by trying to acquire traits that they did not truly understand. A person may try to achieve humility but simply end up with low self-esteem, or try to eradicate anger but end up indifferent to any negativity.

Rav Kook's approach to personal growth was to first clearly define a character trait, and only afterward to try to embody it. A strong definition of what one is trying to achieve helps to arrive at one's aim.

In this chapter Rav Kook will challenge us to rethink seemingly obvious categorizations of good and bad traits. He will show us that what appears to be one trait can actually be its exact opposite; so much depends on the individual and the circumstances. This may be his main lesson in personal growth: to thoroughly understand the goal before pursuing it.

Define the Character Trait You Seek

Misleading Character Traits

There are two steps in sifting through one's *middot* (character traits):

1) A person must develop the ability to distinguish between good and bad character traits and learn how to channel each character trait for its proper use. The ultimate goal is that a person will be able to call on any character trait at the moment that it is needed.

2) A person must develop the ability to break apart and cleanse each individual character trait.

It is true that the superficial understanding of positive character traits is a good start to personal growth and draws one closer and closer to perfection. However, there are character traits that are naturally confusing and misleading. When one is unclear about the definition of a certain character trait, one will be led to traits that seem similar to it, even though they are negative and do not accomplish one's goals. Therefore, a person needs to develop the ability to break apart a character trait and carefully express it with none of its possible flaws. (MA 3.1)

The Reason We Confuse Character Traits

There are several reasons that a person misunderstands the definition of a character trait. One reason is that certain traits seem identical on a superficial level. Therefore, if one truly desires to attain a certain character trait, one must clearly understand and define it. If one does not clearly comprehend that character trait, one will come to a superficial and extreme version of it. Therefore, it is of utmost importance that one investigates each character trait until one can distinguish between its real definition and that which is actually unrelated to it. (MA 3.1)

Why *Teshuvah* Does Not Always Work
As long as a person has not developed the ability to distinguish between the true definition of a character trait and a false one, *teshuvah* will not come about. (MA 3.1)

Confronting "Bad" Character Traits
When one senses a bad character trait in one's heart, one must be careful not to immediately wage war upon it and try to uproot it, for perhaps one will actually need the benefits of this character trait in another area of personal growth. Indeed, one must not assume, based on a superficial first glance, that a character trait that seems negative is indeed so. Rather, this is what one should do: if upon first glance a character trait seems negative, one should contain it, conceal it, and clothe it with Torah values and good deeds. Under this ancient protection, a person is then able to grow toward the good, purifying and filtering out the bad. And as time goes on, a bright light will organically reveal a good character trait. And through the path of education and personal learning…a person will uncover new insights that will guide one to express these "bad" character traits in a healthy way. They will then be elevated to the realm of holiness. (SK 2:194)

Humility

Humility versus Low Self-Esteem
Humility is undoubtedly a good personality trait when a person understands what it is and how to correctly embody and internalize it. However, a misunderstanding of humility can lead to depression because the two are externally similar.

Happiness and arrogance both spread out and expand one's spiritual strengths, but happiness accomplishes this in a good way, while arrogance does this in a bad way. Humility and sadness both gather in and calm one's spiritual strengths, but humility does so positively while sadness does so negatively.

Even though these traits are externally doing the same thing, in essence they are totally distant from each other. When one believes in the enormity of one's own value and thinks this makes him worthy of great things, but then finds flaws or imperfections in oneself that seem to contradict this belief, one will be completely depressed, although there is no truth in this.

Humility, on the other hand, is caused by the recognition that a person's value and ability to accomplish or receive great things are unrelated. Rather, all greatness and goodness that comes one's way are results of the kindness of God flowing down upon this person. Therefore, even when one feels lacking, one will not be sad at all. One will rather thank God for the few good things one still recognizes in oneself and will even be energized to acquire more skills and wisdom. Since this person sees that even in one's seeming unworthiness, God still showers down such kindness, then certainly one will be able to acquire even more greatness within and without. (MA 3.1)

The Danger of Teaching Humility

When we teach people the idea of being humble before God, but we do not explain to them the principle of divine greatness, we damage their souls because we have trained them into a life of slavery and lowliness. Therefore, we have an obligation to first teach people about the principle of divine greatness, so that they will understand that humility before God should naturally give birth to spiritual empowerment. Indeed, if all realms of the world…are one great entity, then when each small element connects itself to the divine whole, it automatically becomes empowered. (SK 1:870)

True Humility versus False Humility

I am in search of true inner humility. Not only will it not hold back the soul's strength, spiritual joy, the development of its talents, and the increasing of its light, but it will actually be the source and motivation for these virtues. "It is beneficial to be humble of spirit" (Mishlei 16:19). (SK 6:216)

Praising Oneself

When *tzaddikim* (truly righteous people) praise themselves, they are actually filled with a great sense of humility. (KYK 2, Pinkas 5:144)

Sadness

Two Types of Sadness

There is a lesser type of sadness that one must push away immediately, without going through analysis and explanation. And then there is a greater type of sadness that comes from the heart of wise people…which demands perfection. This type of sadness recognizes the depth of negative actions and feelings…and it is pained over all types of physical and spiritual suffering. This type of sadness does not need to be pushed away, but rather guided toward its inner purpose. (SK 3:70)

Sadness Shows You What to Fix

My heart will never give up due to any sadness in the world. For I know that this sadness comes to reveal to me a measure of imperfection in the soul, whether it be a fault due to a personal issue or one that is caused by society. Sadness comes to expose areas of pain in order to help repair and shine light into one's actions, ideas, and imagination. (SK 6:215)

Excessive Materialism Causes Sadness

We see that the tendency toward excessive materialism, separating the material from the spiritual and making it the central point of all things, brings one to deep sadness. This is because doing this blocks out the light, the source of life, in every material object, and the soul is strangled by the lack of air. (SK 1:359)

Alienation from One's Essence Causes Sadness

One's misguided actions and beliefs are responsible for the overwhelming sadness that exists in the world. When one is alienated from one's essence – whether physically or spiritually – one becomes enveloped in a damaging mindset that crushes one with continuous waves of negativity. True healing must come through spiritually realigning oneself. When one's beliefs are realigned, one's actions will realign as well. One will begin to feel the value and beauty of life, and the soul will overflow with the happiness of alignment. (SK 1:358)

Sadness Due to Idealism
There is a type of sadness that comes from the soul's deep and holy yearning for ultimate good. Since the more one pursues this, the more one sees how far away it is, one becomes filled with despair. To be sure, this is not the same as the gloomy sadness that is caused by numbing one's heart and seeking that which is external to one's true desires. Instead, this type of sadness has its foundation in a deep inner light that tends to blind due to its intense illumination. However, when one learns to absorb the brightness within this type of sadness, one is redeemed from darkness to light. (SK 8:26)

Anger

Anger That Makes You Lose Perspective
With great anger, but in a calm and controlled way, we must despise the type of explosive anger that corrupts one's intelligence and undermines all the virtuous qualities of human beings, individually and communally. When we see any sect or group continuously speaking with anger, it is a clear sign that these people have lost perspective. They have no meaning with which to fill their emptiness. In truth, they are really just angry with themselves. It is their ego that causes them to project their venomous anger on others. The most profound thinkers who have reached the heights of justice and kindness are filled with never-ending tolerance. Kindness and truth crown them all day long. (OK 3, p. 244)

External Anger

> It is permissible for a person to act angry in order to create an atmosphere of respect in the home. (*Shabbat* 105b)

Anger is poisonous when it lives in the depths of the soul. It is like an alien god within a person's own body. However, actions that seem like anger but are actually being done for a good purpose do not contain the destructive quality of anger. In fact, they demonstrate one's self-control, for one who is required to perform an action that is similar to a deed motivated by raging anger – yet can control oneself and channel the action toward an ethical goal – is one who is truly praiseworthy. (EA, *Shabbat* 2, p. 269)

Holy Anger

> Rabbi Yochanan said in the name of Rabbi Shimon Bar Yochai, "It is permissible to fight with wicked people in this world, as it is written, 'Those who abandon the Torah praise the wicked, while those who observe the Torah fight the wicked' (Mishlei 28:4)." (*Berachot* 7b)

One may think that it should always be forbidden to fight another person, since this is usually motivated by the negative character trait of anger. However, expressing anger at evil by fighting with the wicked is not merely correct, but a highly ethical and intelligent act.

Therefore, it is good to acquire a correct intellectual hatred of evil, even though this involves a form of anger on a personal level. (EA, *Berachot* 1, p. 35)

Jealousy

The Danger of Jealousy

Each spiritual path is unique. Each world is a world unto itself. From one's own world, another person's unique path may appear to be a wasteland of darkness, even though for that person it is truly full of productivity and light. Therefore, each person must be very careful to clarify the boundaries of one's own world. If one decides to take a peek into another person's world, one must be careful to protect oneself. One must only take a peek, and not linger in another's world for too long, for one may uproot oneself from one's own world; and one cannot be absorbed into a strange, new world.

It is possible to be a guest in another's world momentarily, but in trying to establish one's home there, one will find oneself living among scorpions, constricted and isolated in darkness. As it is written, "Why, my son, should you stumble with a strange woman?" (Mishlei 5:20). "Drink water from your own container, flowing water from your own well" (Mishlei 5:15). (SK 5:152)

Jealousy of Others' Talents Leads to Depression

One can sometimes fall into despair upon hearing of some great talent that one is lacking. One can begin to think of oneself as nothing; depression will begin to darken the shine of one's soul. Indeed, one's entire spiritual identity becomes gloomy when comparing oneself to another person who possesses talents that one lacks. And therefore, a person must strengthen oneself and not be jealous of someone else's portion.... One must learn to be truly happy with one's own portion. (SK 2:330)

Holy Jealousy

"Jealousy of wise people increases knowledge" (*Bava Batra* 21a). Without jealousy of wise people, one would only be motivated to imagine, learn, and create that which one is naturally drawn toward. This brings great blessing with it, since the greatest beauty comes from directing one's efforts toward one's own inner drives and talents. Nevertheless, richness and complexity are formed in a person as a result of having access to many different beliefs and ideas. Jealousy of wise people motivates immersion in beliefs toward which one is not naturally drawn, and thereby wisdom increases in the world.

At the end of days, knowledge will become so advanced that the world will be perfected through the unification of all ideas and expertise. Humankind will reach a state where one will no longer have to be jealous of another's knowledge in order to advance one's own wisdom. (SK 4:84)

Arrogance

Why Do We Seek External Approval?
The less self-worth one feels, the more one will seek external approval. Only when one feels lowly in one's soul does one desire to be admired and praised by others – both for what one has and also for what one does not have. Therefore, one has a responsibility to increase one's sense of self-worth. As a consequence, one's language and relationship toward oneself and others will be adjusted appropriately. (MR, "Kavod" 4)

Arrogance Ignores Introspection
When one ignores the negativity inside oneself, does not focus on improvement, does not recognize the ugliness of that negativity, and then believes oneself to be righteous… this is the essence of arrogance.

However, when a person works on self-improvement at all moments – to transform the bad to good, the bitter to sweet, the darkness to light; to honestly feel the spiritual pain inside; to be aware of one's own imperfections – such a person is considered a master of introspection. (SK 6:254)

Arrogance Destroys Desire for Improvement
Arrogance deadens a person's will. And when one's will is weak, no potential goodness can become actualized. (MR, "Ga'avah" 7)

A Cure for Arrogance?
Recognition of arrogance is itself a cure for arrogance. (MR, "Ga'avah" 6)

When Arrogance Meets Low Self-Esteem
Extreme opposite character traits become intertwined when arrogance reaches its peak and one believes oneself to have reached ultimate perfection. One no longer feels the need to search and strive toward any greater excellence. This causes the soul, the nature of which is to always search out its true value, to feel empty and worthless. Due to the poison of arrogance, one lacks the value called the pursuit of growth, and consequently, life loses its purpose. In order to fill this great emptiness, one begins to search for approval from others. Thus, the exaggerated sense of one's own greatness actually brings one to low self-esteem. One chooses to be enslaved by the reactions of one's surroundings and will go to extreme measures to please others.

But this effort will achieve only a superficial approval from others, and it will not be long before even that effect wears off completely, unless the desire to win the approval of others becomes internalized to the point that a person entirely loses a sense of identity, and along with it, all sense of self-worth. (EA, *Shabbat* 2, p. 90)

Holy Pride
One must analyze the feelings of pride that exist inside one's soul and learn to distinguish between arrogance, which ruins one's relationship to oneself as well as to God, and self-confidence, which expands one's mind and reminds oneself of one's spiritual significance. It often happens that one's heart is flooded with confidence, which at first glance appears to be arrogance. Yet when examining the feeling, one will find that it is instead the filling of one's soul with divine assurance.

If one attempts to distance oneself from this "arrogance," not only is one doing nothing for one's soul, but one will also cripple all of one's spiritual strengths. This will lead to depression, and one will believe that this depression is closeness to God when it is in fact ultimate distance from Him. (MR, "Ga'avah" 25)

Holy Self-Love
One's love for oneself can express itself in an unsophisticated way and become corrupted, motivating evil actions and creating bad character traits. The greater one's talents and abilities, the more this destruction of oneself will bring about destruction to the world. On the other hand, love for oneself can be holy and ideal. It all depends on how much one perfects one's mind, feelings, and actions. For when one improves oneself and one's good side grows and fills one's entire being, one's perspective on reality becomes illuminated with joy, because one is looking at the inner value of all things. And reality truly is good when the person looking at it, living it, and acting within it is good. (SK 1:115)

The Emergency Need for Holy Pride
When one feels so weighed down that one cannot even take the smallest step toward growth, it is necessary for one to rise up through the trait of holy pride. One must look at oneself in an entirely positive way and find the good qualities inside all of one's flaws. For when one focuses on searching for one's good qualities, one's mistakes are immediately transformed for the good. In fact, one begins to find so many good qualities in oneself that one becomes overjoyed, and every day will bring the multiplication of one's positive actions. (MR, "Ga'avah" 26)

Beware of False Humility
Sometimes a person will become extremely confident because of an influx of holy pride. It is at this moment that such a person is at the level of the holy of holies and speaks words of fire. In this state, one becomes furious at any low spirit that tries to feed one with false

humility. For in truth, this confidence is filled with humility that is combined with strength, happiness, and a love of seeing everyone succeed. (MR, "Ga'avah" 27)

Freedom

External Freedom versus Inner Freedom
The difference between slavery and freedom is not merely a matter of external status, whereby one person is imprisoned to a master, while another person is not imprisoned. For it is possible to find an intelligent slave whose spirit is full of freedom, and it is also possible to find a free person who has the spirit of a slave.

True freedom is when a person or nation is driven by an exalted spirit to stay true to the inner essence and divine image within. One then feels that one's life is motivated by a greater purpose that is aligned to one's true self. On the other hand, one who lives a life that does not relate to one's inner character is filled with the spirit of slavery. One is then driven by that which is good and pleasing to whomever one views as authoritative. Nevertheless, we must journey toward the inner light of personal freedom. As it is written, "'Engraved on the tablets' (Shemot 32:16) – do not read *charut* (engraved), but rather *cherut* (freedom)" (*Tanna Devei Eliyahu Zuta* 17). (OR 2, p. 245)

Submission Is Not the Ideal Religious Trait
The great visionaries experience the highest level of freedom. They are unable to be involved in any form of submission, because all types of submission are really submission to human beings. In fact, even accepting the kingship of heaven in the usual way the masses do is a form of submission to human beings. The understanding of the kingship of heaven has fallen from its ideal state, and its light has become darkened by human beings' limitations. The ultimate yearning for freedom is the ideal version of *teshuvah* (spiritual growth). (SK 2:160)

7

Listening to the Inner Child

"Amassing more knowledge and wisdom is not what makes us happy. The key to happiness is rather the simplicity of childhood. It is our own good fortune that our culture involves us so heavily in children's education."

MANY PEOPLE PERCEIVE CHILDHOOD AS MERELY PREPARATION for adulthood. All they see when they look at children is small beings who must be taught, formed, and corrected until reaching adulthood. As adults, they should be serious, responsible, and realistic. Based on this idea, the goal of education is to help transition a person from the flaws and imperfections of childhood into the well-roundedness and propriety of adulthood.

Yet Rav Kook rejected this negative understanding of children. He couldn't accept the condescending belief that adults are superior to children in all areas. In fact, Rav Kook believed that adults have much to learn from children.

In this chapter, Rav Kook will explain to us the profound spiritual importance of respecting children in general, as well as protecting one's own inner child.

What Is Unique about a Child?

Children Are Naturally Idealistic
The purity of a child contains within it universal purity. The desire for a life of natural purity pulsates within a child without any dirt or contamination. The holy expression of a pure child includes within it the most powerful and clear spark of the idealism of life. And through this holy expression, it is able to bring the life of the world to its actualization. Therefore, "the world is sustained on the breath of children" (*Shabbat* 119b). (SK 6:284)

The Purity of Children
The natural purity of one's soul can be perceived during childhood. It is in this time period that a person's soul has not yet become contaminated by the madness of life, "the fermentation in the dough" (*Berachot* 17a). We see how easy it is for a child to be receptive to spiritual emotions. At such an age, a person is truly sensitive to holiness and awe of heaven. Therefore, the greatest experts of education have begun to reach the conclusion that religious education, which combines strong intellect and sensitive emotions, is the most natural education for a child. (MR, p. 32)

Childish Ideas Change the World
We must always begin from the start, from the earliest thoughts of childhood. We must attempt to understand them, purify them, and to uncover the good inside. We must be careful not to degrade simple ideas. In fact, these ideas will bring more light to our lives than any supposedly sophisticated idea. (SK 1:351)

Guarding the Purity of Children
The desire and understanding of children are pure. The natural seeds of their knowledge are very healthy. Education must focus on protecting this healthy seed of the child more than it must help

to develop it. Only when the main goal of education is focused on guarding the purity of a child... will all later development be beneficial. The thoughts of faith, the illuminating awareness of Divine greatness, the relationship to God, the certainty of God, the depth of purity and honesty; these are all qualities of a child....

The word of the living God, the foundation of culture, the key to our souls, and a successful society, are all dependent upon children. This is the secret that the Jewish people discovered in exile, and it is because of this that the Torah flourished in exile: the importance of child education was placed as the highest priority. As Jewish nationalism grows, it will need to return to this foundation of life in all of its holiness and strength. (SK 2:258)

When Children Teach Adults

The world is always searching for more knowledge, understanding, and intricate wisdom. Yet at the end of the day, most of our life is focused on the future, on the education of the generation; and education is all about the children. But since the intellectual capability of children is so simplistic and undeveloped, most of the expansive and sophisticated knowledge that adults have attained cannot be absorbed into their minds.

Perhaps we need to learn from this that amassing more knowledge and wisdom is not what makes us happy. The key to happiness is rather the simplicity of childhood. It is our own good fortune that our culture involves us so heavily in children's education. This connection alone attaches us to childhood and all of its purity, and an energy of simplicity is channeled through us and becomes internalized because of this. It cleans out the contamination and crookedness of sophistication that has seeped into us in adulthood. Blessed is the person who draws energy from the sap of childhood even in adulthood. Blessed is one who is like a one-year-old child, free of sins, even after living many ordinary years of life. (SK 7:205)

Grow Up without Losing the Inner Child

What Is the Goal of Child Education?

There is an ongoing question concerning child education: Are we simply training a child to become an adult? Or does the period of childhood have its own intrinsic worth?

If we think that life revolves around having a career and working, then childhood does not have any intrinsic worth. Based on this attitude toward life, a child is simply a pile of clay that is waiting to be formed into a strong and efficient worker. Yet such an approach to education is not correct when one perceives that the ideal life is one that embodies purity, ethics, kindness, and innocence. According to this perspective, childhood is not merely a time when we train a person toward adulthood. Rather, it is a stage in life that has its own intrinsic value. In fact, a person's childhood often becomes the symbol of the highest quality of living that one spends all of one's adult years attempting to regain. This is the deeper meaning of the statement "the world is sustained on the breath of children" (*Shabbat* 119b).

To be sure, even though childhood is good, pure, and holy, it, too, has its weak points. It does not contain the capability to confront many of the trials of life. Therefore, this is our responsibility: to protect the innocence and purity of childhood, and to facilitate a slow transition of all of its shine and innocence into adulthood. This process should be done in such a way that the personality of the educator only contributes the physical and spiritual strength and discipline that the child lacks. The personality of the educator should never be allowed to destroy the precious characteristics of childhood. This is the goal of Jewish education: "at one hundred years old like a twenty-year-old, and at twenty years old like a seven-year-old" (*Bereishit Rabbah* 58:1), "like an innocent one-year-old" (*Yoma* 22b). This is the ideal vision and responsibility of our people's educators. (MR, p. 230)

Before Rav Kook first arrived in Israel, religious people warned him of the strongly secular atmosphere that existed in the city of Yaffo. Nevertheless, Rav Kook made a conscious decision to live there. Here is Rav Kook during his time as the Rabbi of Yaffo, 1904–1914.

Protect the Inner Child

Children's basic senses develop long before they acquire the ability to understand the world intellectually. This happens so that they may experience the world without any of the negative influences of small-minded people. It is essential that a child first encounter the world in its original form without any explanations – first to experience, and only afterward to comprehend. Children must encounter the greater world with no comprehension so that they have a pure foundation from which to begin operating their minds. At first, they must have no explanations and intellect. They must face the world as it is: the work of the Creator's hands, with His enormous power of infinite understanding. All of this should be experienced in the heart of a person from the very moment one enters the light of life. And only once this healthy seed has been planted will the seed of spiritual life endure.

Any natural yearning a person has toward an idealistic dream is really a return to one's inner child. Within this yearning exists an attachment to an ideal that is devoid of any abstract justification. There is an impulse that comes from a place that is totally unconscious. And it is precisely this inner child that we must guard from all negative influences. The innocent awakenings of the soul that come from the purest and most natural part of the spirit must be respected. Yet at the same time, we must be careful to nullify any distorted alien influences. "The prophet who has a dream, let him tell a dream; And he who has My word, let him speak My word faithfully. What is the chaff compared to the wheat? These are the words of God" (Yirmiyahu 23:28). (SK 2:359)

Transitioning from Childhood to Adulthood

Passion is the source of life. In a profound way, we may say that the passion of humanity is the secret principle to transforming the world. However, this passion needs to be developed and matured more than any other personality trait. In its infancy, a natural passion may need an education of conformity, obedience, and compliance. But as one develops, one's inner passion also develops and becomes directed toward the good in a natural way. At this stage, to crush one's passions will only lead to damage and loss.

Transition from one stage of growth to the next is extremely complex and delicate. During this transition, so many passions are wild and out of control. At this point, having restraint and self-discipline is beneficial for one's development. However, so many of one's passions are full of light and goodness. The world's very progress depends on a person staying true to these good values. An honest self-examination will help guide one in this complex process. One must allow oneself to remain true to one's good passions that have already been matured. On the other hand, one's immature passions still require guidance. (SK 1:191)

8

Prayer

"A person who thinks that prayer changes God's will is blaspheming, while a person who thinks that prayer only changes oneself undermines the worth of prayer and all types of religious acts."

UNTIL MODERN TIMES, THE MAJORITY OF MANKIND LOOKED TO God to take care of all their needs. "In God we trust" was entirely literal, encompassing daily life. With the scientific revolution, mankind found a new type of faith: "In man we trust." Belief in one's own self was a protest against the passive faith of a religious era that took no responsibility for change in the world. The modern era proclaimed that not God, but rather man must be the redeemer. If modern man were still to pray, he would pray to himself. Indeed, many new self-help gurus advise their students to repeat self-motivating triggers to awaken a confidence from within.

Are these the only options? Pray to God in total passivity and vulnerability, or rely only on the powers of our own minds and beliefs? What is the function of prayer in the modern era?

In this chapter, Rav Kook explains how prayer works and its relevance in modern times.

What Is the Goal of Prayer?

You Cannot Influence God's Opinion

There is an absurdity to the common understanding of prayer: one prays to God, Who is the most powerful of all beings, and through God one achieves one's desires. God is influenced by the speech of man – He is made to fulfill the requests with which one pressures Him. Is there any blasphemy, disrespect, confusion, or lie greater than this? Should we really be surprised when we see people who are part of a sophisticated society, who consider themselves wise and honest followers of the Torah, yet despise prayer? Just as prayer can be full of darkness when it is devoid of wisdom and emotional intelligence, so too can it be enlightening and uplifting when understood with keenness and sensitivity. (OTf 1)

Praising God Won't Change His Mind

When prayer is oversimplified, it becomes a mockery and suffers the pollution of idolatry. One calls out to God, Whom one imagines as powerful, tough, mighty, and dominating, as One Who pursues honor and forced obedience from His ministers and servants, and Who will likely be won over by lowly people who plead with Him. Then, He changes His authoritative will and fulfills their demands, which are not necessarily virtuous, but rather unsophisticated desires for things that are pleasant, and sometimes things that are unbecoming. This type of prayer is invalid; it is absurd and idolatrous. It lacks the essential meaning of prayer, and it is considered an unintentional offense. (OTf 1)

The Goal of Prayer Is to Transform Oneself

The goal of prayer is not to change the will of God, since God cannot be subject to change. Instead, the goal is to be uplifted by the changes that happen to one during prayer so that one will be in line with the will of God.

While it is true that the person praying speaks to God as a ruling king who can be convinced, or a father who is open to change, or a righteous man who would give charity due to the request of a poor person, this is just a tool so that when the one who is praying yearns to elevate oneself to the Divine, one naturally and already has become one with God's will.

Regardless of the act of attaining that which the person praying requested, prayer is in and of itself a powerful tool in perfecting an individual. The manifestation of the request is simply a result of that transformation. Therefore, each person praying should understand that the act of prayer is a miraculous law of nature that God created in His world for the purpose of bringing His creatures to every type of perfection.... It must be made clear: prayer is not something that influences God, Heaven forbid. (OR, "Tefillah" 2.2)

Does Prayer Change the Person or God?
A person who thinks that prayer changes God's will is blaspheming, while a person who thinks that prayer only changes oneself undermines the worth of prayer and all types of religious acts. However, a person who believes that by changing oneself, one changes the world – since all of existence is influenced by the transformation of one of its elements – this understanding of prayer will bring blessing to one's soul and the entire world. (SK 1:664)

Prayer Is Not Magic; It Actually Affects You
Prayer is one of the most practical ways of attaining one's desires – spiritually and physically, communally and individually. The ideal type of prayer is when a person is also actively involved in practical ways of attaining one's desires; prayer is then connected to real ways of actualization....

Prayer that is filled with a spirit of laziness is not the ideal prayer. This is a sign that the great benefit of prayer has not been internalized in the depths of one's soul. One is still filled with doubts and questions that frustrate the weakened heart concerning the essence and importance of prayer. And even if a person battles against these thoughts and decides to believe in prayer, for this person it is merely a magic trick. One's faith in the power of prayer is weak; it is still not understood as a natural law of the universe.

Therefore, a person must lift oneself up to an inner understanding of the power of prayer and connect all actions taken toward any goal with prayer. (SK 4:92)

Why Are People Uninterested in Prayer?
The main reason people in our generation are uninterested in prayer is that the focus on practicality has strengthened within the Jewish people... and too often prayer is associated with the old-fashioned idea of weakening one's desires. As a consequence, this generation does not appreciate its power and beauty. Therefore, it is our duty to uncover the light within prayer, the hidden goodness of strengthening a person's desires. Once we do this, many people will return to prayer. (SK 1:73)

Prayer Causes Transformation
Prayer causes an actual transformation inside a person, and one's inner transformation eventually builds up and leads to a revolution in the entire world. This is specifically evident when both the inner and external elements are directly connected. (SK 1:851)

Prayer Actualizes Your Hidden Desires
Inside one's soul exist many positive desires. Yet one must learn to actualize them. The best way to do this is through speech, which influences one's mind and imagination. Therefore, prayer is very important; it brings out our deepest emotions. (SK 1:33)

Confused versus Focused Thoughts
Every day, one needs to purify, cleanse, and elevate one's imagination. It is prayer that helps one achieve this goal. It is impossible to imagine how much dirt and waste is flowing around in the soul of

an individual, a nation, humanity, and the entire world. Only by letting go of the impurity can one cleanse and refine one's imagination.

The imagination is easily influenced by negative impulses. It can quickly descend to the lowest lows; that is, unless we try to elevate and refocus it constantly. This is why we are in need of blessings and prayer in a regular schedule. Fortunate is the person who says them with deep concentration. Prayer will enlighten both oneself and the entire world. (SK 1:66)

The World of Optimism
Prayer is an absolute necessity for oneself and for the entire world. The waves of the soul rush back and forth, demanding from both oneself and from the entire world a type of perfection that the limited world simply cannot provide. As a consequence, one finds oneself left with a constant feeling of sadness. It is a frustration that may even cause one to lose one's mind.

However, before it is too late and this cancer is allowed to spread inside, we begin to pray. We pour out our words and are elevated to a world of ultimate perfection. When doing this, our own inner world visits this perfected world. We become filled with a peace of mind. At last, the inner force that affects the universe, of which one's inner self is an element, transforms the world to a place of optimism. (OR, "Tefillah" 1.7)

Light in a Dark World
Prayer challenges the soul to actualize its purpose. When many days and years have passed by without a powerful prayer, stones gather up within the heart. One begins to feel a heaviness of spirit. However, when the wind of good spirit returns, and the gift of prayer is given from above, those stumbling blocks are removed.

As the soul experiences a state of elevation during prayer, one's past becomes healed. Of course, this will not happen all at once.

Instead, one starts to grow and the light of prayer guides one and reveals one's own path. (OR, "Tefillah" 1.3)

Inner Transformation Changes the World

When one's spiritual consciousness is transformed and a new divine insight begins to shine in one's soul, the external world takes on a new form. It is like the creation of a great artist. The world is new and full of beauty, with all of the negativities of one's old world passing and fading away. This new reality isn't simply a subjective experience; rather, the more truth contained in this transformation, the more it really does transform and beautify the world. (SK 4:33)

Prayer Reveals the Unconscious Self

Prayer takes the hidden part of one's soul and actualizes it. The effect of prayer when it rises up from the depths of the unconscious self will depend on the extent of the purity of one's inner world. (OR, "Tefillah" 1.4)

The Power of Speech

Self-Transformation through Spoken Words

Saying words out loud has a powerful effect on one's life. When a word is spoken, great light emerges with it. The deeper one pierces into the words of prayer, the greater the power of light that they will bring and the more influence they will have to create change. The clearer the expression, the clearer the light and the more focused its effect. The words become reality, and it is impossible that prayer will have no result. (OR, "Tefillah" 1.4)

The Energy of a Word

Every word spoken opens a channel to the soul in accordance with its value. Therefore, each word of Torah, wisdom, and morality... opens a doorway to the outpouring of holiness. The waves of the soul are constantly being moved through the tremendous power of speech.... On the other hand, an empty word, and all the more so a negative and hurtful word, opens an impure channel to the soul. Many waves of mud and dirt pour through, until eventually a spirit of goodness returns and cleanses it.

Any word that is drawn from a person's inner desire for holiness – even when it appears to be in simple conversation – is really sourced in the inner essence of a person's will. Therefore, when people have a deep vision... every conversation that comes from their spirit opens up channels of goodness.... As it is written, "The simple conversations of *talmidei chachamim* (people learned in Torah) must be studied" (*Succot* 21b). In fact, some of these are equal to the entire Torah. (OK 3, p. 281)

Transforming the World via Speech

When one's soul is elevated, one begins to feel the incredible power of speech. Such a person truly understands the significance of every spoken word, of every prayer and blessing, of every teaching and conversation. This person perceives the great importance of all forms of speech and senses how the development of the world and all of its changes are a result of speech. (SK 6:246)

The Spiritual Power of Screaming

The sparks of holiness that dwell in the depths of negativity are what cause a person to scream out, so that the entire body experiences it. Now, as long as one is sensitive to the holy sparks within, one's actions and speech will be calm and respectable.... However, if one needs to suddenly raise up these sparks of holiness from the bitter depths, then screaming out loud is very helpful.

There are *tzaddikim* (righteous people) who cry out loud to God due to the sufferings and general tragedies of the world. This type of cry will continue until the world is filled with perfection and light. The cries of these *tzaddikim* do not come from their inner spiritual destress, but rather from the great sufferings of the world – the sufferings of the Divine Presence, which screams like a mother giving birth.

And just as a small piece of wood is able to set fire to a large piece…so too, a small scream is able to cause a great spiritual and intellectual awakening. A yearning fire – a divine thirst – burns inside one's soul, but it needs an external force to draw it out into the world. And sometimes with just a tiny action, something powerful is produced. (OK 3, p.287)

What Should One Pray For?

To Remove Evil and Reveal Light

When one requests something in prayer, one must be careful that one's intention is to remove evil and darkness from the world and to strengthen divine good and light. In fact, when one's request is motivated by this intention, not only do one's own mistakes become corrected, but also all mistakes and faults are in some way improved. What we seek is an all-encompassing perfection. (OR, "Tefillah" 2.4)

To Pray for Oneself or for Others?

> Rabbi Yosi said in the name of Rabbi Chanina, "Prayer was established by the Avot (Avraham, Yitzchak, and Yaakov)." Rabbi Yehoshua ben Levi said, "Prayer was founded in place of the sacrifices." (*Berachot* 26b)

True service of God is when a person perfects oneself, when one connects to God with all of one's heart and soul. It is nevertheless true that the purpose of self-perfection is to eventually improve the Jewish people, and finally to fix the world in the Kingship of God. Although prayer is connected to the deepest and most personal emotions of the heart, it is mainly built on many national dreams: redemption, a righteous government, the Mashiach, the rebuilding of Jerusalem and the Temple….

Therefore, our question is as follows: What was the main reason for the establishment of prayer? Perhaps the outpouring of the soul is the main point, and the national dreams are a mere outgrowth and consequence. On the other hand, perhaps the central goal is national perfection, and the individual soul naturally becomes purified as a result.

When the Avot were serving God, there was no Jewish nation in the world. Thus, the main focus was personal growth without any connection to one's people. In contrast, the sacrifices were the service of the nation. Therefore, the opinion that says prayer was established by the Avot challenges us to serve God through the spiritual development of the individual, whereas the opinion that says prayer was founded in place of sacrifices challenges us to serve God through the Jewish people. (EA, *Berachot* 1, p. 109)

How Should One Pray about Enemies?

> Our rabbis taught, "Shimon Hapakuli wrote the eighteen blessings in their order before Rabban Gamaliel in Yavneh. Rabban Gamaliel said to the Sages, 'Can anyone among you write the blessing about the evil person?' Shmuel Hakatan came down and wrote it." (*Berachot* 28b)

The blessings of our prayers are filled with kindness and love. Any truly wise person is able to write such prayers for a holy and intelligent people. However, a prayer that includes within it matters of hatred and anger must be written specifically by a person whose heart is totally pure and holy, harboring no real hatred. When this person prays to God to destroy evil people, it is because those people are preventing God's greater goal from being actualized. However, if one has even the smallest amount of personal animosity toward evil people, then even if one is initially focused on God, one's emotions will eventually lead one to an increased hatred that is improper and illogical.

Therefore, Shmuel Hakatan was the only one who was qualified to write the blessing about evil people. He was the person who always said, "When your enemies fall, do not rejoice" (*Pirkei Avot* 4:19). He removed all the hatred from his heart, even toward his adversaries. We thus find in his blessing only pure intentions for the actualization of God's greater purpose. (EA, *Berachot* 1, p. 121)

How Can God Reply to Prayers of Enemies?

Perhaps your heart asks you: If many people are praying for their own individual needs, and all the nations are praying for their own successes, victories over their enemies – then how can God listen to everyone when some of these prayers contradict each other?

You should answer: Prayer is accepted based on how much it is aligned to divine purity and honesty.... The more a prayer is filled with righteousness... the more it will have influence. Some prayers actualize half of their desires; some produce a third or a quarter, or even one percent. It all depends on the worth of the prayer in accordance to God's measurements. (SK 7:114)

Preparation for Praying

Exhausting versus Energizing Prayer

> Rabbi Eliezer says, "When one makes one's prayer '*keva*,' one's prayer is not considered sincere." What is "*keva*"? Rabbi Yaakov the son of Idi said in the name of Rabbi Oshaya, "A prayer that feels like a burden." (*Berachot* 29b)

Before praying, one should feel as if one's soul is weary and exhausted from the burden of worried thoughts that are so distant from perfection. Only through pouring out one's words before one's Creator and Father in heaven is one able to remove from the heart this burden. Through prayer one is given courage, and instead of a worrying spirit, one will be crowned with happiness and the strength and joy of God. However, when one has an incorrect understanding of prayer, it lacks this energy and can itself exhaust a person. Prayer must be motivated by an inner driving emotion and not some external obligation, for then it would necessarily be "a prayer that feels like a burden." (OR, "Tefillah" 2.3)

How Depression and Laziness Affect Prayer

> Our rabbis taught, "One should not pray when feeling depressed or lazy." (*Berachot* 31a)

Prayer comes to awaken the soul's potential to focus on pure thoughts. Yet it also comes to awaken the body's potential to focus on moral actions. Therefore, one must prepare both physically and spiritually in order to achieve from prayer its intended goal. In order not to hold back the soul from its transformation, one must not be in a state of depression, which prevents the soul from ascending to pure and clear thoughts. One must also avoid being in a state of laziness, so that the body is open to being aroused toward moral actions. (EA, *Berachot* 1, p. 129)

Don't Bow Too Much

> A person is only allowed to bow at the beginning (Avot) and end (Modim) of the Amidah. But if one desires to bow down at the beginning and end of every blessing, we must teach him not to bow. (*Berachot* 34a)

One should not bow down too much, because one must recognize one's own divine greatness and talents. Only then will one be able to lift up one's heart in the path of divine service. Therefore, "if one desires to bow down at the beginning and end of every blessing, we must teach him not to bow." (EA, *Berachot* 2, p. 164)

The Inspiration of Beauty

> Rabbi Eliezer says, "When one makes one's prayer *'keva,'* one's prayer is not considered sincere." What is *"keva"*? Rabbi Yaakov the son of Idi said in the name of Rabbi Oshaya, "A prayer that feels like a burden." The rabbis say, "Whoever does not say it in the manner of supplication." Rabba and Rav Yosef both say, "Whoever is not able to insert something fresh into it." Abaye bar Avin and Rabbi Chanina bar Avin both say, "Whoever does not pray at the first and last appearance of the sun," for Rebbe Chiya bar Abba said in the name of Rebbe Yochanan, "It is a religious duty to pray with the first and last appearance of the sun." Rabbi Zeira further said, "What text confirms this? 'They shall be in awe of You with the sun and before the moon throughout all generations' (Tehillim 72:5)." (*Berachot* 29b)

The world around us should naturally awaken our emotions to pray. One's heart should be awakened to pray Shacharit (the morning prayer) by the wonders of God that can be seen in the rising of the sun. One should be aroused to pray Minchah (the afternoon prayer) by the wisdom and kindness of God's presence that can be seen during sunset.

When a person is inspired to prayer at the very moment that the world itself is changing, one's prayer is not criticized as being *"keva."* One's emotions at this time are no longer focused exclusively on one's own inner world, but instead have expanded to be sensitive to the universe as a whole. One begins to see the divine kindness that fills everything. However, when one disconnects one's emotions from the moments of life that should naturally lead to feelings of inspiration, then one's prayer is called *"keva."* One has become indifferent to the greatest praise of God: the spectacular wonders of the universe.

"They shall be in awe of You with the sun and before the moon throughout all generations" (Tehillim 72:5). What does this verse mean? Through praising and being conscious of the laws of nature, one will arrive at an awareness of God. This is in line with the prophets' words: "Raise your eyes on high and see Who created these things" (Yeshayahu 40:26). Thus, every person with an understanding heart should take opportunities to encounter God through the wondrous universe that is always giving praise to its Creator. (EA, *Berachot* 1, p. 124)

9

The Spiritual Importance of Creativity

"I walk around with an overwhelming jealousy of the secular world. It is a jealousy that consumes me. For is it really possible that the power of creativity has ceased within the religious world?"

WHEN RAV KOOK WAS THE CHIEF RABBI OF ISRAEL, HE OFTEN MET with famous political figures. Yet it seems that he was more interested in his meetings with inspirational musicians, poets, and authors. Over time he developed a strong relationship with some of the most influential Israeli Jewish poets and writers, such as Bialik and Shai Agnon.

Immersing himself in their exciting novels and poetry, Rav Kook was deeply moved by their use of creativity. He noted that there sadly existed no parallel to these popular secular writers and artists in the religious world.

If Rav Kook were alive today, he might put it like this: Why is it that inspirational secular musicians sing their songs to fifty thousand people at a time in enormous stadiums all around the world, while the deepest and most profound spiritual ideas are often ignored or unheard of? In other words, why is the religious world so far behind in the development and use of creativity?

In this chapter, Rav Kook will explain to us that before we can translate religion for the people of the twenty-first century, we must begin to understand the spiritual importance of creativity.

Creativity Is a Spiritual Value

Jealousy for the Secular World
I walk around with an overwhelming jealousy of the secular world. It is a jealousy that consumes me. For is it really possible that the power of creativity has ceased within the religious world?... Has it all been given over to the secular world? How could this be? To begin addressing this problem, we must reexamine our actions and beliefs. It must be an honest criticism, whether positive or negative, concerning all realms of our spiritual life....

My constant pain is a jealousy on behalf of the holy. A piercing pain stabs my heart when I see secular thoughts and dreams spread throughout the world, winning people's hearts, acquiring followers, and eventually becoming actualized in concrete deeds, whereas dreams and thoughts of holiness are left alone like a dead stone that no one picks up or notices. There is no one who is willing to explain, expand, and help the world appreciate these holy ideas. Nor is there anyone who is striving to help actualize them into practical deeds. And thus, concerning all of this I become sick and suffer great pains of the soul. These are my sufferings of love that cause me to call out in a great voice to proclaim a spiritual revolution. (C, pp. 215–17)

Develop a Spiritual Appreciation of Art
In order to overcome the chaotic destructiveness of atheism, we must educate religious people to be physically healthy as well as spiritually healthy. We must help them develop a refined sensitivity and awareness of the beauty of emotions. This is possible only through the involvement in the wonderful beauty that exists within music, poetry, nature, and all of the arts. "A beautiful home, a beautiful spouse, and beautiful furniture expand the mind of a person" (*Berachot* 57b). (OE, p. 17)

"I Truly Think Rembrandt Was a *Tzaddik*"
When I lived in London, I used to visit the National Gallery. My favorite pictures were those of Rembrandt. I truly think that Rembrandt was a *tzaddik*. Do you know that when I first saw Rembrandt's works, they reminded me of the legend about the creation of light? We are told that when God created light, it was so strong and penetrating that one could see from one end of the world to the other. However, God was afraid that the wicked might abuse it. What did He do? He reserved that light for the righteous to use when the Mashiach would come. But now and then there are great men who are blessed and privileged to see it in their lifetime. I think that Rembrandt was one of them, and that the light in his pictures is the very light that was originally created by God. (*The Jewish Chronicle* [London], September 13, 1935, p. 21)

Poetry Clarifies the Meaning of Life
Faith is the poetry of life, the poetry of reality, the poetry of existence. A poem gives us the most profound insight, the deepest and most penetrating understanding of an idea, which dry words could never capture. Therefore, the most authentic perspective of life is specifically within the poetic side of life, and not in the mundanity that can be described in prose.

Woe to those who want to strip their lives of the beauty of poetry; they will lose all the depth of life and all of its inner truth. Prose itself only has meaning insofar as it is rooted in the poetry of life. (SK 1:165)

The Purest Song
There is not a song in the world that does not contain some light of holy faith. However, a truly holy song is one in which holiness reveals itself in the spirit of music in its purest form. Only ministers of holiness, ministers of God, sing such a song. (SK 8:179)

Exaggeration That Is Really Truth

Tzaddikim (truly righteous people) see the world in all its greatness, and therefore will sometimes exaggerate. Yet they are actually telling the truth from their perspective on the world, which is really the more profound perspective. "How great are the creations of God; how deep are Your thoughts" (Tehillim 95:6). (KYK 2, Pinkas 5:145)

Poetic Eyes See Spirituality in Everything

If you will, human being, look at the divine light inside everything. Look at the heavenly life, and how it spills into every direction and corner of reality. The divine light is in the spiritual as well as the physical. It stands before the eyes of the body as well as the eyes of the soul.

Contemplate the wonders of creation. Look at the divine life within them. Do not perceive the universe as a faded image that is placed in your line of vision from afar. Rather, you must be familiar with the reality in which you live. Know yourself and your world. Know the thoughts of your own heart and of every visionary and philosopher. Find the source of life that is within you, that is beyond you, and that surrounds you. Know the glory of life of which you are a part.

You must take the love inside you and elevate it to its powerful, refined, and beautiful source. Expand this love to all of its branches, to anything that has the soul of life inside. It is only the fault of the perceiver that causes the light to appear diminished. Look into the lights and into their essence. Do not let the descriptive names swallow your soul. Indeed, the words and letters are given into your hands; you are not given into their hands.

Rise up higher and higher. You have enormous strength. You have spiritual wings. You have the wings of a powerful eagle. Do not deny them, or they will deny you. Seek them and they will find you immediately. (OK 1, pp. 83–84)

We Must Encourage Creativity

Are You a Poetic Soul?

Those who possess poetic souls must be aware of their own unique personality traits and pay careful attention to their individual desires and yearnings. One must be conscious of the special movements of one's soul, and of the particular spiritual diet that is required to nourish it. This spiritual nourishment is as vital to the poetic soul as oxygen is for breathing.

Even if such a person is forced to be associated with other types of knowledge (including other religious subjects) to which one is not drawn, one must never forget that one must stay true to one's own unique and independent spiritual foundation. And one must approach every type of work, conversation, or religious or academic idea from one's pure and powerful soul that is filled with a holy song. (OK 3, p. 215)

Write Down Your Inspiration Immediately

It is a very important thing to watch one's thoughts and imagination, and to write down every idea as soon as it is born in the depths of the soul. One must watch over it as it comes from the hidden realms to the revealed light, and record all the impressions that one feels along the path of its development. (SK 8:52)

A New Spiritual Language

A letter to Rabbi Yitzchak Levi (secretary of Merkaz HaRav Yeshiva and one of its co-founders), September 26, 1913

I want to encourage you and all the youth who seek to be immersed in a life of spirituality... concerning the development of writing. We must acquire for ourselves the skill of writing; it must be in a style that is full of life in all of its different forms – both informative and poetic. If there is one among us who feels an inner pull toward song and poetry, please do not neglect this talent...

Now, even though I am always telling myself and others that the most important character traits we must have are peace and kindness, we must nevertheless be prepared for the spiritual war – the inner and external Amalek. We must arm ourselves with the weapon of our time: the pen.

In order to attract the people of our generation, we must translate all of our holy writings – the principles and emotions of almost the entire Torah – into a modern language. This can be compared to Ezra the scribe, who modified the words of the Torah. One of the main reasons he did this was in order to help his generation draw closer to understanding it....

An enormous collection of spiritual writings is inaccessible, and it is our responsibility to draw from them each day and translate them into a modern language.... We must utilize the daily and weekly newspaper, *HaMoriah*. We must not take for granted any opportunity to put words of truth and charm into a book. (IR 2, pp. 225–26)

A Yeshiva Should Teach Creativity
Letter to Rabbi Yitzchak Halevi Herzog (Rav Kook's successor as chief Ashkenazic rabbi of the land of Israel), August 1, 1908

... I'm not saying that all people in yeshiva should be experts in all realms of thought. Obviously, this is above most people's ability. Only a few *yechidei segulah* (unique souls) are born with the talent of absorbing knowledge from all perspectives, while the majority of people can only become experts in a specific area. As it is taught: "A person only learns that topic which his heart desires" (*Avodah Zarah* 19a).

Yet despite all this, a yeshiva is obligated to give to the Jewish people anything it lacks. And since one of the main things that is drawing people's hearts and having a great effect on our generation is creative literature and poetry, we must therefore also make sure that we have religious experts in this field.

Indeed, it should not be an accepted fact that every talented writer and famous poet is an atheist or one who has already given up his religion. We must break this stigma and show the world the poetic beauty that comes from those who are immersed in the source of the nation's natural life, from those who are faithful to God, the source of the waters of life. (IR 1, p. 195)

Letter to the Bezalel Art School
A letter to the Bezalel Academy of Arts and Design, 1908

There are people who say that creating a school of Jewish arts should not be a priority at this present period of time. They say that there are more urgent and important issues.... Nevertheless, a desire that comes from the heart of its people, this very yearning, is a sign that there is life and hope for success.

Yet this sign of life is not just a hollow symbol. It may bring many practical benefits. The development and growth of Jewish art will bring financial profits to many Jewish families living in the land of Israel. "And its fruit will be for food and its leaves will be for healing" (Yechezkel 47:12).

In addition, it will help develop emotions of beauty and purity for the children of Zion.... It will lift up many depressed souls and help give them a clearer and more enlightened perspective on the beauty of life and nature, and the importance of work and agriculture. (IR 1 p. 204)

The Official Ideology of Bezalel Art School

> To train the people of Jerusalem in crafts, develop original Jewish art and support Jewish artists, and to find visual expression for the much yearned-for national and spiritual independence that seeks to create a synthesis between European artistic traditions and the Jewish artistic traditions of the East and West, and to integrate it with the local culture of the Land of Israel. (http://www.bezalel.ac.il/en/about/landmarks/)

Boris Schatz (1866–1932), founder of the Bezalel Academy of Arts and Design, in 1906. Schatz was so appreciative of Rav Kook's support that he gave him a tapestry as a gift. Rav Kook immediately hung it on the wall for all to see in the main room of his house, where it remains until this day.

A Revival of Jewish Spiritual Books

A letter to Rabbi Dr. Moshe Seidel (professor of Bible studies at the Rabbi Isaac Elchanan Theological Seminary and one of Rav Kook's closest students), October 21, 1908

It is very important to me that there should be a strong and loving connection among our society of spiritual seekers. We are people who realize that there is a new and enormous spiritual job ahead of us.

The spiritual elements of the Torah (*aggadah*, Midrash, Jewish philosophy, and kabbalah) must be focused on with at least the same amount of energy that is given to the practical parts of the Torah (Tanach, Mishnah, Gemara and *halachah*). This is surely one of our future goals. We must begin to write down the thought processes, the questions and answers, of the principles of faith. They must be expressed with clear logic and emotional intelligence.... All this must be written specifically by people who live in the world of Torah.

While it is true that there do exist people in our generation who have already written about these matters, most of these writers have left Judaism for a secular life. Therefore, these people are not able to fully comprehend the hidden and eternal light of Torah and Judaism. When it comes to matters of the practical sides of the Torah, all the seekers of our generation have been able to turn for advice to the answers of the ancient rabbis. Indeed, in matters of practicality, there is clarity in most of the details. We must do the same with the intellectual and emotional intelligence of the spiritual elements of the Torah. The spiritual principles will rise above, shed light, and bring life to the practical details. Therefore, I want to begin a regular correspondence with all the spiritually seeking youngsters, who know the Torah and love it.... Together, we must begin to revive the abandoned world of Jewish spiritual books.

Yet according to how important the matter is, so too will be the size of the obstacle.... But I will not despair. I put my hope in God, who gives us the light of the world... to help me actualize my dream. And that phrase that I have become accustomed to saying will finally be fulfilled: "From the thoughts of my mind, matters will be gathered and expressed into letters and words. They will then be transformed into essays, chapters, and finally books that will be distributed."

We must sing this song together. And from the four corners of the land of Israel these songs will be heard. Indeed, the joy of God will be our strength. (IR 1, p. 213)

How Spirituality and Creativity Inspire Each Other

Teshuvah as a Trigger for Poetic Writing
The inner struggle of *teshuvah* is enormous creative material for the singers of heartbreak and the weavers of tragic stories. It awakens their instruments and reveals their creative talents. (OT 8:10)

The Mashiach Will Be a Poetic Writer
The beautiful and profound emotions of *teshuvah* (spiritual transformation) must be revealed though creative writing. This is in order

Shai Agnon (1880–1970), great Jewish writer and Nobel Prize laureate. Agnon had a deep respect for Rav Kook. He would often visit Rav Kook's house to talk about spiritual matters. When asked why he never wrote a novel based on Rav Kook, Shai Agnon replied, "I could never do him justice."

that our revolutionary generation will understand *teshuvah* in the depths of their soul in a new and fresh way. People will come back to Judaism and be healed. A singer of *teshuvah* will rise up. This person will be a singer of life, a singer of revolution, and a singer of the national soul that is currently being redeemed. (OT 17.5)

From Shai Agnon's Nobel Prize Speech

> As a result of the historic catastrophe in which Titus of Rome destroyed Jerusalem and Israel was exiled from its land, I was born in one of the cities of the Exile. But always I regarded myself as one who was born in Jerusalem. (http://www.nobelprize.org/nobel_prizes/literature/laureates/1966/agnon-speech.html)

Something Inside Pushes Me to Write

I am always fighting this inner battle: a powerful spirit is pushing me to speak about *teshuvah*. All of my thoughts are focused toward it. Indeed, *teshuvah* takes up the biggest part of Torah and life. All of our individual and collective hopes are built upon it. *Teshuvah* is a mitzvah that is, on the one hand, one of the simplest mitzvot, since even a fleeting thought of *teshuvah* is already considered *teshuvah*. On the other hand, it is one of the hardest mitzvot since it is never completely materialized in this world.

I find myself constantly thinking and speaking about *teshuvah* and nothing else. So much has already been written about it in the Torah, Nevi'im, and the words of the ancient rabbis. Yet despite all this, *teshuvah* is still unclear and requires elucidation. The creative writing that exists in every realm where there is song and life has still not penetrated the depth of *teshuvah*. It has not even begun to pay attention to it and to understand its nature and worth. It has not developed its endless poetic nature, and certainly has not touched the surface of its practical side.

I feel a push from within to talk about *teshuvah*. I am frightened by my own thoughts: "Am I indeed worthy of speaking about *teshuvah*?" The greatest thinkers of past generations – the purest prophets and rabbis, and the holiest Chasidim – wrote about *teshuvah*. And how can I stand in their company? Nevertheless, I will not allow any weakness in the world to exempt me from my inner obligation. I am forced to speak about *teshuvah*. Specifically, I must give voice to both its poetic and practical sides. I must help our generation understand its depth and guide us to actualize it in our individual and collective lives. (OT, introduction)

Betzalel as a Role Model for Artists

> Rabbi Yehuda said in the name of Rav that Betzalel knew how to combine the letters of the alef-bet that created the heavens and earth. As it is written, "Betzalel was filled with the spirit of God, with *chochmah* (intellect), *binah* (understanding), and *da'at* (wisdom)." And then it is written, "God created the earth with *chochmah* and the heavens with *binah*." And then it is written, "With God's *da'at* the earth was opened and the sky was filled with dew." (*Berachot* 55a)

The true talent of artists emerges when they have reached such a state of consciousness that the spirit of God inspires their artistic expression. They are then able to perceive the depths of both the physical and spiritual nature of the universe. In fact, all character traits that are attributed to the Creator of the universe must also be found in the wisdom of great artists.... In order for Betzalel to have designed the Mishkan, he must have been inspired by the spirit of God. He had the *chochmah* (intellectual ability) to design the physical structure, *binah* (an understanding of the spiritual purpose), and the *da'at* (wisdom) to apply these physical and spiritual ideas in the most precise and intricate details (EA, *Berachot* 2, p. 126)

A Description of a True Jewish Author
It is impossible for a Jewish author to truly be successful without the soul first going through a spiritual transformation. Any writer who does not focus on purifying his or her character traits, actions, and thoughts... cannot be called a true writer. One must have the combination of an inner world that is overflowing with light and emotional greatness together with a desire to perfect one's own flaws....

"The ancient rabbis were called *sofrim* (writers, but also means "counters") because they knew how to count the letters of the Torah" (*Chagigah* 15b). By counting the letters of the Torah, they were transformed into people who synthesized a humble spirit with self-confidence, and thus they deserved the title of "writer." Therefore, if we truly desire to revive Jewish literature, we must return to this holy path. We must learn to connect the world of holiness to the world of writing. As it is written, "There will be a path; and this path will be called holy.... And those who walk down this path will be redeemed" (Yeshayahu 35:8–9). (O, "Hatechiyah" 36)

Creativity Must Be Moral
There will come a time when every poem and every poet will be spiritually transformed. The world will then become aware of the great

power and value of poetry. This will lead to the spiritual advancement of the world; the light will expand and break out. Sensitive souls, who recognize the impure values in many poems, will protest against any lyric that covers up its negativity with a superficial line of kindness or bright melody.

This impure spirit, like all types of impurity, will pass away and be destroyed from the world. Beauty will take its place, and poetry will be spiritually transformed. Every poet will begin to understand the great and holy value of his or her poetry. A person will not pick up a pen without first cleansing the soul and elevating the thoughts. Reflections of *teshuvah* will precede any new creation.

Only then will creativity be expressed in its full purity. The spirit of God and the soul of the nation will be manifested through poetry. A time will come when immoral poetry will be despised, and the Jewish people will finally say: "'As for Me, this is My covenant with them,' says God. 'My Spirit, which is on you, will not depart from you, and My words that I have put in your mouth will always be on your lips, on the lips of your children, and on the lips of their descendants – from this time on and forever,' says God" (Yeshayahu 59:21). (O, "Hatechiyah" 37)

Rav Kook spent his entire life trying to inspire the people around him. He was known for being a charismatic public speaker.

Creativity Should Be Effortless

It is impossible to stifle creativity in a person whose soul is constantly creating from its source. When a person feels restricted by a sense of mental fatigue, it is a sign that one perceives one's creation as an act of work and labor. Yet the more one delves into the essence of creativity, the more one recognizes that there is no work and labor. God created the world with absolutely no effort and labor. Therefore, the more one emulates God, the more one is able to create without experiencing a feeling of exertion.

The purest *tzaddikim*, the holiest people, rise beyond the consciousness of any work and effort. Even though they are certainly willing to work hard, suffer, and sacrifice... for the sake of fulfilling God's will, nevertheless, they are always filled with a peace of mind, and the energy of delight fills their holy souls constantly. The wellspring of intellectual and emotional inspiration swells and pours into them from all directions. Whatever they listen to and feel, "everything calls out God's presence" (Tehillim 29:9). "Everything calls out holy, holy, holy, the legions of God fill the earth with His presence" (Yeshayahu 6:3). Then, creative freedom and all its blessings expand within one's mind and heart.

At every moment, new worlds are created and formed. Past worlds that were once created disappear and are recreated into a newer, higher, holier, more sophisticated and beautiful form.... There are no feelings of fatigue, restriction, labor, or work. Rather, one experiences only peace and joy. "And I will rejoice in God. I will be joyful in God, my Savior" (Chavakuk 3:18). (OK 1, p. 168)

What Motivates Me to Write?

An open letter addressed to all of the youth of Israel who love Torah, 1905

I write not because I have energy to write, but rather because I do not have enough energy to be silent. (IR 1, p. 24)

The Second Song
The Song of the Nation

10

Ethics and Concern for Others

"It is forbidden for the fear of heaven to push away the natural ethics of a person. And if it does do this, then it is not a pure fear of heaven."

IS RELIGION MAN'S QUEST FOR GOD? INDEED, IT SEEMS AS THOUGH religion is an attempt to solve the deepest spiritual problems of life. Perhaps achieving a state of *devekut* (oneness with God), a type of spiritual enlightenment, is the ultimate goal of religion.

Yet religion becomes dangerous when it becomes purely focused on God. Do we not see many "religious" and "God-fearing" people all around the world who commit murder, violence, and acts of immorality? We are desperately in need of a religious voice that focuses on the holiness of man at least as much as the holiness of God. What does religion have to say about interpersonal relationships?

In this chapter, Rav Kook focuses on the spiritual importance of one's relationship to others.

True Spirituality Motivates Ethical Courage

The Ethical Goal of Religious Education
Letter to the editor of *Havazelet* (a Jewish newspaper published 1863 to 1911), November 8, 1908

The goal of education is to give one the tools to actualize one's ideal self; its main focus must be to transform one into a compassionate and honest person. From the ancient days of Avraham calling out to God, we have inherited the principle that the more one is connected to God, the greater will be one's compassion and honesty; it will lead to greater individual and social well-being. (IR 1, p. 218)

Moral Religion versus Immoral Religion
It is forbidden for the fear of heaven to push away the natural ethics of a person. And if it does do this, then it is not a pure fear of heaven. In fact, the sign of a pure fear of heaven is when natural ethics – which is planted within the honest nature of a person – grows and develops to even higher levels than it would have without it. If without one's fear of heaven, a person would have desired to do good toward individuals and the community, and only because of its influence, this force of good has been lessened – then this fear of heaven is invalid. (OK 3, introduction, p. 27)

Ethics and Spirituality Must Be Connected
It is crucial for a person to develop natural ethics in all its depth and breadth, and a fear of God (in other words faith) in all its depth and breadth. The highest spiritual qualities of one's soul can only be built on both of these entities. (OK 3, introduction, p. 27)

Speaking versus Living Faith
There is more faith and connection to God found in intellectual honesty and good ethical traits than in words spoken about faith and emotional images. (SK 1:231)

Spirituality Must Bring Heaven Down to Earth

Human civilization is too narrow for us. Our souls are so great that we seek to affect all of existence. Our morality desires to care for all creatures, for all of existence. And therefore, this desire must be actualized through the words drawn from the Master of all existence. The Torah of Israel must be taken from heaven and drawn down to earth. It is the deepest talent of this nation to harmonize the heavenly light, so that it is completely connected with the materialization of higher ethics....

"You are in this world, and You are in the next world" (from the words of the Siddur). These two worlds must not be separated. The details must not be disconnected from the highest ideals... The light of the endless One must not be removed from the smallest and most detailed problems that need to be fixed. (OK 3, p. 3)

Growing Up

A person's life can be split up into two halves. In the first half, one must perfect oneself by developing physically as well as spiritually (Torah, intellect, and morality). By the time the second half has arrived, one must already be trying to affect and influence others. By using one's talents to help those who are less developed, one assists them in their own paths toward improvement. (EA, *Shabbat* 1, p. 35)

Finding Oneself by Caring for Others

One must always try to transcend one's individual world. Sometimes self-centeredness fills one's whole being, until all of one's thoughts are focused only on one's own individual concerns. This way of thinking undermines a person's greatness and will eventually lead to both physical and spiritual suffering.

Instead, one must dedicate one's thoughts and desires to the greater good: others, the nation, and the entire world. And (paradoxically) through doing this, one will come to know one's own essence. (OK 3, p. 147)

Rav Kook developed strong friendships with many influential political figures. Here, Rav Kook is pictured with Mordechai Eliash, Israel's first ambassador to the United Kingdom.

The Universal Soul

Letter to Rabbi Shmuel Alexandrov (a great Jewish philosopher, mystic, and writer who perished in the Holocaust), May 28, 1908

All our limbs are connected organically. Therefore, when one limb suffers, all limbs suffer. This connection can also be felt within a spiritual unity of connected souls. This is the organism in which a family is founded. These senses can become so real and concrete that if we dedicate ourselves to transcending our habitual way of thinking, we realize that there is a connection of pleasure and pain just as from one limb to another between a father and son, a husband and wife, etc.

When these connections expand, our sensitivity will also expand. When the national organism is healthy, each of its members feels connected to it in the same way relatives feel connected to a family. When one develops this connection, the self expands to the level of one's nation. The next step is from the national to the humanitarian level. And yet one more step is from the humanitarian level to all of creation. The final stage moves from an interest in the earth to a deep concern for all of existence. All of this only takes time. Indeed, though it may take a lot of time, eternity has no need to rush.

This sensitivity can continue expanding until one has ascended to an individual consciousness of all existence. If this is true, then there is no danger of anarchy in a great self-love that is refined and sophisticated. It is Judaism's goal to give us a practical way of life that is rooted in the individual consciousness of the source of all worlds. (IR 1, pp. 174–75)

Accepting the Other

Long-Lasting Peace

When we look at the world, we see so many differences of opinion. We see such stubborn disagreements between individuals and groups of people. Indeed, the more one becomes convinced of one's own opinion, the more intense these disputes will be.

Yet a person who tries to look deeper will realize that these arguments are like two seeds planted in soil. The distance between the two seeds is necessary in order to allow for each seed to be watered, nourished, and grown in each one's optimal way. Whereas planting them too closely together would actually have disrupted and ruined both, the distance between the two allows for each plant to flourish.

Sincere and long-lasting peace only develops from giving each other space. "Those who dwell separately will eventually unite" (*Zohar*, Mishpatim 95a). (OK 1, p. 15)

Accepting That People Are Different from You

Here is an important principle in life: one must live according to one's internal moral intuition, both in thought and in action. One must not focus on the fact that others, with their differing character traits and personalities, do not act in the same way as oneself. Neither should one put down one's friend or think negatively of another for being different from oneself.

A person must be careful not to degrade a personality trait or action in a friend that would be destructive and unbecoming for oneself. One should not be so quick to judge that things are the same for another person. Perhaps that which would have been a point of embarrassment for oneself is for a friend not only harmless, but actually beneficial.

Concerning one's attitude to oneself: one should never think that because another behaves in a certain way, and because this is a person one admires, that it therefore must follow that one should copy this person's path in serving God. No! This is not true. Indeed, one may perhaps discover that if one tries to walk down the same path that suits one's friend, one will at best attain only some superficial resemblance, and may in fact become damaged instead. Therefore, a person must be true to oneself, and at the same time judge others favorably and accept them for who they are. (KYK 1, Pinkas Rishon l'Yaffo 49)

The Spiritual Importance of Disagreements

> Rabbi Eliezer said in the name of Rabbi Chanina, "*Talmidei chachamim* [Torah scholars] increase peace in the world, as it is written, 'All of your children are students of God, and there will be great peace for your children' (Yeshayahu 52). Do not read the words as *banayich* [your children], but rather *bonayich* [your builders]." (*Berachot* 64b)

There are those who make the mistake of thinking that world peace will come about when everyone agrees on one opinion. Then when they see that the more *talmidei chachamim* learn, the more opinions are created, they begin to believe that these people are causing more conflict rather than creating peace.

But in truth, in order to increase peace, all the different views and opinions must be articulated. It must be explained how each opinion has its own unique role and function. While on the surface they may seem to contradict each other, when each side's wisdom is truly and deeply expressed, we realize that only by combining different opinions can the light of truth, righteousness, and wisdom of God be truly conveyed.

"*Talmidei chachamim* increase peace in the world." The explanation is as follows: the very fact that they explain, clarify, and give birth to new ideas of Torah from different perspectives is what creates peace. As it is written, "All of your children are students of God." Everyone will eventually understand that even the seemingly contradictory opinions are "students of God." Each opinion uncovers a different truth of God. Do not read the words as "your children," but instead, "your builders." Just as a house is built from different parts, so too is truth built from the combination of different perspectives and ideas. "These and those are the words of the living God" (*Eruvin* 13b).

Indeed, each unique method of education has its own role and function. Thus, it is wrong to abandon or throw away any idea or viewpoint. One must invest energy into each side and try to understand its role. And when two opinions are found to be in contradiction, it is precisely through this clash that wisdom is created. (EA, *Berachot* 2, p. 361)

The Danger of Criticizing Others

We must examine the nature of those who want to improve others and try to force them to change. Perhaps a certain path is actually good for another person, even though it has its flaws. These flaws may in fact be protecting that person from even greater dangers. May God guide us to be fair. Sometimes we are tempted to enter a mode of criticizing everyone, but this is completely insensitive. We must be compassionate; and when one has compassion on others, God forgives all faults. (MiR, "Tochacha")

Letting Go of Superficial Labels

When Religious Categories Destroy Religion

We often imagine that the Jewish people are split up into two groups. There is this never-ending echo we hear of two names that make up our people: religious and secular. These are new names that in our long history we have never pronounced. Of course, we have always understood that people are not the same, specifically in regard to their inner spiritual nature, but to allocate a separate and distinct name to identify an entire group is entirely new. There is no doubt that the past was better than the present in this regard, and how much better off would we be if we could forget these two names....

The pronouncement of these two names and the imaginary agreement that connects certain people together, so that one person will exclaim, "I am from this group," and another will say, "I am from this group," each one feeling pleased with their division, is what prevents any growth and development on either side.

The "religious" person – that is, the person who thinks he belongs to the group that calls itself "religious" – looks down from a high podium at the secular group. Concerning matters of change, improvement, and *teshuvah*, he aims his critical eye at the other group that stands before him naked of Torah and mitzvot. He thinks in his mind that improvement only applies to "them, and not him" (quoted from the Pesach Haggadah's response to the Wicked Son).

The "secular" person – that is, the person who thinks he belongs to the group that calls itself by this modern name – thinks that this entire concept of *teshuvah* is "religious" and therefore does not apply to him. Alas, from both sides we stand frozen. From where will the cure to our spiritual sickness come?

We have no other choice but to wipe out these two idolatrous names from among the Jewish people. We are not used to two names, but rather three. There is an ancient tradition that the word *tzibbur* (congregation) includes *tzaddikim* (righteous), *beinonim* (average people), and *resha'im* (the wicked). Nevertheless, this allocation of names is only for the sake of the individual's assessment of himself. Therefore, it is most beneficial for each individual to take a personal accounting and purify one's own flaws while looking with a favorable eye toward others. (MaR, pp. 76–77)

Rav Kook always opened his heart to the many visitors of Israel. Here he is pictured with some tourists in his Jerusalem house.

Jewish Unity: Religious and Secular

Concerning the disagreement on how to run the nation: As the secular have increased overwhelmingly, and the religious do not want to have anything to do with them, perhaps we should split the nation into two. Or, on the other hand, perhaps the power of national unity is what will overcome all problems....

This can be compared to the famous story of the two women who came to King Solomon. When the king of Israel said, "Bring me a sword," he truly had divine wisdom. The mother who said, "Kill the baby," proved to us that she was the fake. This bitter statement expressed what she was really feeling inside: "Neither you nor I will get the baby – therefore kill!" The compassionate mother, the true mother, said, "Give her the living child, just do not kill." It was *ruach hakodesh* (divine wisdom) that proclaimed, "Give the living baby to her, for she is the true mother."

There is nothing worse than splitting up the physical and spiritual into separate parts. In fact, this is the worldview of idol worship. (O, "Hatechiyah" 20)

Spiritual Peace

We must be more involved in bringing spiritual peace between different ideologies than in bringing physical peace between people. In fact, only spiritual peace will bring physical peace. (KYK 2, Pinkas 5:35)

The Orthodox Label Is Too Narrow
Letter to Agudat Yisrael (a political party representing *charedi* Jews), May 12, 1912

We must clarify something:... The faithful and holistic Jews who are passionate about God, or as it is incorrectly labeled today, the "Orthodox sect,"... cannot fit into one narrow group within the Jewish people, which is only concerned with its own well-being.... Instead they must be a part of the entire Jewish people, and their main concern must be creating peace within the nation and its ultimate redemption. They must recognize that they are the soul of the nation... and that their role is to pour out the spirit of life upon all the different groups within the Jewish people. (IR 2, p. 78)

Focusing on the Good in People
When we focus on the good qualities of people, an automatic love arises. There is no longer any need for cheap flattery. When we become truly focused on a person's virtues, we become almost unaware of his or her more negative qualities. (OK 3, p. 324)

Love the Good and Not the Bad
One can only explicitly express love to a person who exposes a small spark of goodness. If one attaches one's love to that spark, one can love the good side of another without being damaged by the negative and darker side of that person. (OK 3, p. 317)

Love and Hate beyond Reason
If we and the world around us became destroyed due to *sinat chinam* (a hate beyond reason), then we and the world around us will be rebuilt because of *ahavat chinam* (love beyond reason). (OK 3, p. 344)

11

Zionism

> *"The land of Israel is not just some external object, some material possession of the nation.... Rather, the essence of the land of Israel is tied to the very life of the Jewish people."*

TO BEGIN, WE MUST ASK: WHY BE A ZIONIST? WHY MAKE ALIYAH? Why commit your life to a piece of land in the Middle East? The fear of financial, social, and cultural challenges, terrorism, and sometimes war, make many want to simply ignore the questions.

Herzl's "political Zionism" tried to solve the Jewish problem of anti-Semitism. Achad Ha'am's "cultural Zionism" attempted to solve the problem of assimilation. A.D. Gordan's "labor Zionism" believed the real problem was a Jew's alienation from physical labor. Ze'ev Jabotinsky's "revisionist Zionism" thought the failure of the diaspora was "the weak and vulnerable Jew." Is Zionism merely about running from problems? Rav Kook, while agreeing with many of these points, envisioned a deeper, intrinsic Jewish connection to our homeland.

For many Jews in the twenty-first century, Zionism is not what it used to be. People have lost their passion. The state is built: national parliament, kibbutzim, economy, Hebrew language, and a Jewish army are all already here. Suffering the paradoxical defeat of success, Zionism no longer has the attraction that it used to hold. According to the experts, "post-Zionism" is here, and there is no going back.

In this chapter, Rav Kook brings us back to the most basic questions: Why be a Zionist? Why make aliyah?

What Is So Special about the Land of Israel?

The Land Is Not Just an External Object to Use

The land of Israel is not just some external object, some material possession of the nation. Nor is it just some tool to achieve unity and strengthen our physical and even spiritual existence. Rather, the essence of the land of Israel is tied to the very life of the Jewish people. Consequently, it is impossible to understand the holiness of the land of Israel or our love for it through mere intellectual justification.

Trying to understand the land of Israel as purely an external object that unifies the nation; or as a tool to strengthen Jewish identity in exile; or even as a tool to strengthen faith, fear of God, and practical mitzvot is misguided. The foundations of these understandings are weak compared to the holy power of the land of Israel. (O, "Eretz Yisrael" 1)

Zionism Isn't Only about Solving Problems

Our goal must not only be the redemption from Egypt, being healed from a sickness, escaping poverty and blinding darkness. We must not yearn to simply get rid of negativity. This impulse depresses the soul and gives no meaning to life. God did not create us for this....

Rather, we must yearn to be full of greatness, with joy in our souls, full of renewed life that shines light in every direction we turn.... Toward You, only toward God – it is Your greatness we seek, hope for, and await. To the land of Israel we are coming; for our redemption and the redemption of our souls are we yearning.

It is not about being saved from the chains of exile... No! It is something much greater than this. We are seeking light, the flow of life from the source of the holy of holies... looking toward the holy land, the land of life. (KYK 1, Jerusalem 7)

The founding fathers of religious Zionism, *left to right*: Rav Tzvi Hirsch Kalischer, Rav Yehuda Alkalai, Rav Shmuel Mohilever, and Rav Yaakov Reines

The Ideal Motivation for Making Aliyah

The following is excerpted from a speech that was given by Rav Kook in the Churva synagogue in the Old City of Jerusalem on Rosh Hashanah in September 1933, two years before he passed away. Rav Kook will explicitly mention Adolf Hitler, and therefore it is important to note the following historical context:

– January 30, 1933: Hitler was elected Chancellor of Germany.

– March 22, 1933: The first concentration camp was opened in Dachau, Germany.

– September 15, 1935: The Nuremberg Laws were passed, taking away Jewish rights of citizenship. Jews were no longer allowed to be German citizens, marry non-Jews, or have sexual relations with non-Jews.

"It shall be on that day that a great shofar will be blown, and those who are lost in the land of Assyria and those cast away in the land of Egypt will come, and they will bow down to God on the holy mountain in Jerusalem" (Yeshayahu 27:13).

"May our God and the God of our forefathers blow a great shofar for the sake of our freedom" (from the prayers of Musaf on Rosh Hashanah).

The prophet foretold about the great shofar of redemption. We are praying for the sounding of this shofar – specifically the "great" one.

THREE DIFFERENT SHOFARS

The shofar of redemption has different levels: the great shofar, the middle shofar, and the small shofar.

The shofar of Mashiach is compared to the classic shofar of Rosh Hashanah. Jewish law establishes three levels in regard to the ideal shofar of Rosh Hashanah:

1. Ideally the mitzvah is to use a ram's horn.
2. In a non-ideal situation, a horn from any kosher animal is acceptable.
3. If we have no choice, then although a shofar of a non-kosher animal or an animal used for idol worship is invalid, nevertheless, if one blew from it, one has fulfilled one's obligation. In truth, as long as a blessing is not said, it is permissible to blow from any animal horn when there is no kosher shofar available.

The same levels that were given as Jewish law on Rosh Hashanah correspond to the different levels of the shofar of redemption. When we say the "shofar of Mashiach," we mean the awakening and drive that produces the revival and redemption of the Jewish people.

THE GREAT SHOFAR – SPIRITUAL MOTIVATION

There were times in Jewish history, and even still today, when groups and individuals had an inner drive for total redemption of the Jewish people that was rooted in holiness, in a powerful faith in God and the Torah, in the holiness of the Jewish people and its mission, and in the desire to fulfill God's will.

This is what we mean when we say the great shofar: the lofty desire for the nation to be redeemed so that it can fulfill its great mission, which is not possible in the midst of misery and exile.

THE MIDDLE SHOFAR – NATIONAL MOTIVATION

There are times when the ultimate holy desire becomes weakened and the great, fiery yearning for holiness is absent. Nevertheless, there is at least still healthy human nature, which in truth is also rooted in holiness. A nation naturally desires to establish independence in its own land, to arise and be liberated, to live a life of simple freedom like all other nations. This desire, which comes from a feeling of nationalism, is the middle shofar, which can be found in all places. Although not the ideal choice, it too is a kosher shofar. "In a non-ideal state, a horn from any kosher animal is acceptable."

THE SMALL SHOFAR – ANTI-SEMITISM MOTIVATION

However, there also exists a third level of the shofar of Mashiach. The small shofar, which is normally invalid, is permitted to be blown in a situation of extreme necessity – when a horn of a kosher animal is impossible to find.

When the ideal desire for holiness and redemption has disappeared, when the natural desire of nationalism in a self-respecting people has disappeared, when it becomes impossible to blow a kosher shofar for the sake of redemption, then the enemies of the Jewish people will come and blow for the sake of redemption. They force us to listen to the sound of their shofar. They blast and shriek into our ears, not allowing us any peace or rest in exile.

The shofar of an impure animal becomes transformed into the shofar of Mashiach. Amalek, Petliura, and Hitler awaken the redemption. He who does not hear the sound of the first shofar, or even the sound of the second plain shofar, does not want to hear and has blocked up his ears – but he will be forced to hear the sound of the impure and invalid shofar.

He too fulfills his obligation, because even within the national feeling of persecution is a type of redemption. However, on a shofar like this we do not make a blessing. "We do not make a blessing on anything that is a type of curse" (Mishnah *Berachot* 6:3).

PRAYER FOR THE IDEAL MOTIVATION FOR ALIYAH

We pray that God will not bring us to hear this invalid and impure shofar against our will, nor even the middle shofar, the nationalistic shofar. Rather, we pray, "Blow the great shofar for the sake of our freedom," a shofar that comes from the depth of the holy Jewish soul, from among the holy of holies. Only then will we have a complete redemption. (MaR, p. 269)

Exile Creates a Consciousness of Fear

The most terrible Divine curse in exile is a heart full of fear, as it is written, "And the survivors among you – I will bring fear into their hearts in the lands of their enemies" (Vayikra 26:36). The fear of the heart spreads through one's spiritual life no less than it spreads through one's entire physical life. It damages the former not less, but actually in a deeper way than it damages the latter.

The fear of every "copper button" (non-Jewish law-enforcement officers) has caused us to become ragged, exhausted spirits who are unable to receive the light of redemption and liberation, even when it presents itself to us. The fear of any book that stands outside the narrow realm of the idea of holiness, as defined by exile, weakens our spiritual life. It creates fragile souls that are unable to receive the strength of the spiritual light that will shine upon us like lightning on the road to our revival in the land of our forefathers.

The physical fear of any type of authority suppressed our spirits, and we accepted this as necessary. What could we have done? But "the consolation of Babylonians is like blasphemy" (*Bava Kama* 38a). For a Jew of exile, it is strange, perhaps impossible, to think that there can exist Jewish authority and law enforcers. Organized law enforcement is for non-Jews. This type of thinking has become so entrenched in us that many have come to believe that without non-Jewish guards, the Jewish people would be unable to survive. In any moment of emergency, we must turn only to them, as if they are our shields and saviors.

This is also true in matters of spiritual authority. Although our literature contains everything – *ma'aseh bereishit* (the story of creation) and *ma'aseh hamerkava* (mysticism), *halachah* and *aggadah*, musar, philosophy and logic, solutions to eternal questions – it is believed that it cannot contain the solutions to our present questions. The temporal questions and all the sciences of creation are considered like those authorities to which the Jewish form must bow. However, all of these ideas and those similar to them are merely fruits of exile, consequences of the broken impurity that has poisoned us since we were exiled from our soil and ceased to be a living nation, dwelling in its own land.

The time has come when we need to consider reality and expand our mindset. We are unable to exist now as we existed in the past according to the necessities of exile. There, we threw our hopes to non-Jewish authority, and when we were in need of sciences we turned to non-Jewish languages. Not so in the land of Israel. Here the life of our society and civilization is in our hands, and we need to take control of our material and moral property. We are experiencing a revival, and our language and literature is coming back to life as well. It is possible to ignore this in exile and to deny the reality of this revolution, but not so here, in the land of Israel, where the revival is forcing open our eyes against our will. (MaR, p. 504)

Four Zionists who symbolized the new fearless Zionist Jew, *left to right*: Joseph Trumpeldor, Ze'ev Jabotinsky, Yair Stern, and Menachem Begin

The founding fathers of modern Zionism, *left to right*: Theodore Herzl, Achad Ha'am, A.D. Gordon, and Ze'ev Jabotinsky

Secular, Religious, and Anti-Zionist Beliefs

Passive versus Active Redemption

The knowledge that everything is in the hand of God and for a higher purpose, and the promise that we will return to our foundation, our holy land, is itself what has weakened our practical effort, and caused a deadening of enthusiasm.

As long as there are opportunities to act, there is no reason to be passive, for are not all acts of man in truth acts of God? Nevertheless, the arrival at this understanding requires much preparation and maturing in intellect, in feeling, and in life. We also need to greatly arouse the desire that we ourselves will be the ones to act, as much as we possibly can.

But we have fallen, and we have not risen up. So what does God do? He strengthens the *chutzpah b'ikva d'Meshicha* (audacity in the times of the Mashiach, Mishnah *Sotah* 9:15) so that the masses distance themselves from the depths of knowledge and faith, overstepping all boundaries until the awareness of God within them is silenced. Consequently, the faithful promise of God does not inspire them. Instead, their yearning comes from the longing for comfort from their present persecutions, and even, to a small degree, from the drive to defy faith, Torah, and mitzvot. Nevertheless, this motivation will do its job to ignite their hearts and cause them to move and to act.

In the meantime, those who are religious need to develop an understanding of the holiness of practical actions, until all souls can be uplifted with this knowledge. That which has been accomplished on the basis of forgetting God will then be accomplished even further through awareness of God's desires. (PR 2, pp. 143–44)

Why Is the State of Israel So Secular?

We are no longer able to close our eyes to the lack of influence that Judaism is having on the Zionist movement. This is true both in regard to its spiritual/moral elements, such as education and literature, and also in regard to its practical/physical elements.

We must admit that the main reason for this failure is that the religious community has not taken enough of a role in the Zionist movement. This is despite the fact that some of the earliest Zionists were religious – for example, the Vilna Gaon (1720–1797) and Rabbi Tzvi Hirsch Kalischer (1795–1874) – and there were certainly religious leaders later on during the official establishment of the Zionist movement [Rabbi Shmuel Mohilever in 1824–1898 and Rabbi Yaacov Reines in 1839–1915]. Anyone with open eyes can see that Zionism is the hand of God redeeming His people.

Unfortunately, precisely those who are the most religious have not opened their eyes. This has caused them to become indifferent and apathetic, and they have taken only some insignificant role in building up the land and reviving the nation. Now, as a consequence of all of this, there is no powerful religious influence on the Zionist movement, which should naturally have been enormous, since Zionism is rooted in our holy religion. God forbid that I would say our religious leaders lack faith in general, but unfortunately, when it comes to matters of redemption and returning to the holy land, which the rabbis tell us will happen gradually (Yerushalmi *Berachot* 1a), there is a type of faith that is indeed lacking in the spiritual leaders of our generation.

The Mizrachi movement must take responsibility and repair this weakness of faith, and in doing so revive the great spirit of holiness that is waiting to influence the Zionist movement. (MaR, p. 482)

Why Did Our Generation Merit Redemption?
Some people are asking: What did our generation do that they merited redemption? The answer is simple. Its merit was that it was involved in the greatest of all mitzvot, a mitzvah that is equal to the entire Torah. It was involved in redeeming the Jewish people. In fact, it was not only involved, but it is still involved – and will continue being involved-without a moment's rest – in the redemption of the Jewish people. This divine strength is what is elevating and leading it to salvation. (SK 7:201)

Preparing Material Needs of the Jewish People
The first generation of the coming of the Mashiach that will begin settling the land of Israel will prepare the material needs of the Jewish people.... And when the material strength of the nation has been established, the inner spiritual qualities will be revealed, and the Torah will return with all its powerful light. (SK 1:88)

Who Has the Greater Soul?
The *nefesh* (physical element of the soul) of those secular Jews who are connected with a great love to matters of the Jewish nation, to the land of Israel, and to the revival of its people, is more perfected than the *nefesh* of religious Jews who lack this profound concern for the Jewish people and for building up the land of Israel. On the other hand, the *ruach* (spiritual element of the soul) of those who are religious and follow the Torah and mitzvot is more perfected.

The solution will come only through the Mashiach, who will unify the Jewish people. The *nefesh* of the religious will be repaired with the help of the perfected *nefesh* that is found in holy secular people, in regard to matters of the nation and physicality that are

A classic picture of spiritual yeshiva students *(left)*, versus the new, physically strong secular Zionist *(right)*

understood by human intellect and emotions. On the other hand, the *ruach* of the secular people will be repaired through the influence of those who are religious, observant of Torah, and strong in faith. As a result of all this, a great light will come upon both groups, and a holistic spiritual transformation will emerge in the world. The Jewish people will then be ready for redemption.

The greatest righteous people, the most profound souls, will act as a unifying pipeline through which will pass the light of a corrected *nefesh* from left to right and the light of a corrected *ruach* from right to left. Only then will there be great happiness. "Your priests will dress in righteousness, and your pious ones will sing" (Tehillim 132:9). (O, "Hatechiyah" 43)

Is Being a Zionist a Disgrace to the Torah?
Letter to Rabbi Yaakov Dovid Wilovsky, known by the acronym Ridvaz (a great writer and founder of many yeshivot, the Ridvaz argued with Rav Kook over the proper observance of the *shemittah* year), June 29, 1913

And regarding your criticism of me that I have become a Zionist in my old age, by bringing my soul close to the path of settling the Jewish people in the land of Israel: My good friend, if all Zionists loved the land of Israel and longed to settle it with the intention and holy goal that I have in mind – because it is the land of God that He chose and cherished more than the entire universe, and because it has the ineffable quality of prophecy and the holy spirit, and to merit by walking through it to Olam Haba (the world to come) – if all the Zionists thought like this, it would certainly be a grand honor for every *ga'on* and *tzaddik* (any great person in the Jewish people) to be called a Zionist. (IR 2, p. 194)

Universal Zionism

Three Groups in the Jewish People

There are currently three conflicting forces within our people. The war between these forces is most recognizable in the land of Israel, but their activity derives from the general life of our people, and their roots go back to human nature itself. These three forces need to be united among us so that each will help the other perfect itself. Left on its own, each one will present the distortion of extremism, which is diminished when each one challenges the other. We would be most unfortunate if these three forces should be left in mutual isolation. These are the three basic drives that our life and the life of all humanity must express in some form: religion, nationalism, and humanism.

The strength of each of the three forces varies. Among some individuals, or in some societies, one force may play a greater role than another. But we shall not find any form of human life in which these three are not all present in some way. The harmonization of these great drives must be achieved in every society that desires survival. When we look at our lives and realize that these three forces, despite their need to be united, are actually moving further apart, we must take immediate action....

There are three groups that we currently see in the Jewish people.

One is that which people have grown accustomed to call "Orthodox." It carries the flag of holiness and argues passionately for a life of Torah, mitzvot, and faith.

The second group contains the new type of nationalists, who

fight for all matters that have a patriotic quality. It desires to rebuild national life after so many years spent in the bitter exile. It desires to absorb many of the wisdoms collected from other nations for the sake of enhancing our own.

The third group is that of the liberals. In the past, it was the same group that raised its flag during the enlightenment period. In today's age, it continues to show its influence in many wide-ranging fields. Instead of focusing its effort on national aspirations, it demands universal enlightenment of culture and morality.

However, it must be recognized that in a healthy state, there is a need to combine all three forces. We must always aspire toward a healthy situation in which each force is given the ability to influence us in all its richness and virtue. The ideal harmony comes about when no group is deprived of its influence nor given too much power. The religious, national, and universal should work together in both an ideological and practical form. Each individual and group will begin to realize that it has a unique talent within this three-way coalition. Each group will recognize the virtue and benefit that the other groups provide.

This consciousness will continue to expand and mature until not only will each sect appreciate the good virtue within the other groups... but even more than this... each group will understand the need to be influenced by the criticism of the other group... so that through this critique each one will become balanced and protected from the danger of its own extremism....

And therefore, when we look with intellectual honesty at the controversies that we are suffering in our generation, we must know that there is only one path open to us. Each one, whether individual or collectively, should internalize this lesson: everyone is called upon to defend the unique values to which one feels connected due to the nature of one's soul as well as one's custom and education. But also, one must understand how to utilize the wisdom that is found in other types of people and groups. By doing this, one will be able to balance oneself and one's group.... And through this path we can hope to arrive at a type of life that is fitting for our nation living in our land.

To be sure, we must realize that when we said that the religious is only one part of the three-way coalition, and that it must diminish itself to give room to the other groups, we were only referring to the technical and ritual element of religion.... But the higher level of religion... is free from all restrictions, and connection to God is always filled with expansion that is higher than all limitations. "I saw an end in all finite things, but your mitzvot are all-encompassing" (Tehillim 119:96). And when the individual and nation walk in the ways of righteous actions and thoughts that are measured in their correct boundaries, peace will eventually come about [between the different groups of Israel], so that they too will be able to ascend to a higher form of inclusivity. "I called out to God from limitations and God answered me in expansiveness" (Tehillim 118:5). (O, "Hatechiyah" 18)

Does Universalism Negate Nationalism?
The ambitious desire to love all of humanity in the same way that one loves the Jewish people must be examined and clarified. An understanding of the uniqueness of the Jewish people, which creates a powerful love that spills over to all of mankind, is the strength of Avraham Avinu. He was the father of all of humanity. "Through you all of the people on earth will be blessed" (Bereishit 12:3).

However, sometimes the love of humanity is motivated by a lack of emotional attachment to and awareness of the uniqueness of the Jewish people. If so, it is poisonous, and all actions that grow out of it are destructive. (O, "Yisrael" 8.5)

Betraying One's Own People

> Rabbi Akiva says, "[You should love God] with all your soul" – even if your soul is taken away."

Our rabbis taught: Once the wicked Roman government issued a decree forbidding the Jews to study and practice the Torah. Pappas ben Yehuda came and found Rabbi Akiva publicly teaching and occupying himself with Torah. He said to him, "Akiva, are you not afraid of the Roman government?"

He replied, "I will explain it to you with a metaphor. A fox was once walking alongside a river, and he saw fish going in groups from one place to another. The fox said to the fish, 'From what are you fleeing?' The fish replied, 'From the traps created for us by men.' The fox said to them, 'Would you like to come up onto the dry land so that you and I can live together in the way that my ancestors lived with your ancestors?' The fish replied, 'Are you the one that they call the wisest of animals? You are not clever, but foolish. If we are afraid in the condition in which we live, how much more so in the environment in which we must die!' So it is with us. If such is our condition when we sit and study the Torah, of which it is written, 'For it is your life and the length of your days' (Devarim 30:20), if we neglect it, how much worse off we shall be!"

It is related that soon afterwards, Rabbi Akiva was arrested and thrown into prison. Pappas ben Yehuda was also arrested and imprisoned next to him. Rabbi Akiva said to him, "Pappas, who brought you here?" He replied, "Fortunate are you, Rabbi Akiva, that you have been imprisoned for dedicating yourself to the Torah! Woe to Pappas who has been imprisoned for dedicating himself to foolish things!"

When Rabbi Akiva was taken out for execution, it was the hour for saying the Shema. While they combed his skin with hot iron, he was accepting upon himself the kingship of heaven. His students said to him, "Our teacher, even to this extent?" He said to them, "All my days I have been troubled by the verse '[You should love God] with all your soul' (Devarim 6:5), [which I interpret to mean] even if your soul is taken away. I said, 'When will I have the opportunity of fulfilling this?' Now that I have the opportunity, shall I not fulfill it?" He prolonged the word *echad* (one) until he passed away while saying it. A heavenly voice went forth and proclaimed, "Fortunate are you, Akiva, that your soul has departed with the word *echad*!" (*Berachot* 61b)

Pappas believed that since the Roman government had announced that their hatred of the Jewish people was only due to a spiritual disagreement, all the Jews needed to do to solve the problem was to extinguish the Jewish spiritual light. [Pappas reasoned,] *If we do that, then the Roman hatred will go away and they will eventually allow the Jews to return to their normal life.*

But Rabbi Akiva understood that the Roman government had merely come up with this superficial reason of spiritual disagreements to justify their hatred. In truth, they hated the essence of the Jewish people, a hatred that comes from an evil soul that says, "Only me and no one else" (Yeshayahu 47:8). Therefore, [Rabbi Akiva reasoned] if the Romans had not justified their hatred through a spiritual disagreement, they would have found other justifications. And if they could not find any other justifications, they would have simply oppressed and destroyed the Jews without reason or cause. The truth was finally exposed when the Roman government found justifications for their discrimination even against the Jew who tried to hide his Jewish identity. When Pappas was eventually imprisoned, he became angry and frustrated that he had betrayed his true self in order to win the love of the enemies of his people.

Praiseworthy is the person with a pure heart and a spirit of courage, who is willing to stand up for his people and its Torah even when enemies try to destroy and annihilate them. (EA, *Berachot* 2, p. 233)

Mashiach Ben Yosef and Mashiach Ben David

Mashiach ben Yosef is the attribute of Jewish nationalism. However, the ultimate goal is not a narrow nationalism but rather to unify the entire world to call out in the name of God. Even though this may require a special center, the goal is not the center but its effect on the greater whole.

When the world seeks to transform nationalism into universalism, there must be a form of destruction in those matters that were rooted in shortsighted patriotism, which possesses the deficiency of an overly restricted love. Therefore, in the future, Mashiach ben Yosef will be killed, and the true and eternal kingdom will be that of Mashiach ben David. (O, "Yisrael" 6.6)

Love of One's Own People and of All People
I love all. I cannot but love all people, all the nations. From my very depth, I want the fulfillment of all, the perfection of all. My love for Israel burns more intensely and is deeper. But my inner desire spreads out in the force of its love for all. I have no need to force this feeling of love. It springs directly from the holy depth of the wisdom of the divine soul. (AT 76)

The Honesty to Critique One's Own People
The great love that we have for our people should not prevent us from critiquing its flaws. However, even after the freest critique, we discover that its essence is totally clean of any dirt. "You are completely beautiful, my darling; there is no flaw in you" (Shir Hashirim 4:7). (SK 3:345)

Rav Kook sitting for a portrait in the courtyard of his Jerusalem home, 1934

We Will Never Abandon Our Dream

Only a people who have finished what they started can exit the stage of history.... But to start and not finish, that is something which is impossible. That inner urge, which is so strong within us, to continue Judaism – in thought, action, peoplehood, and land – comes from a deep intuition that we still have to complete what we started. We began to say something great, to ourselves and to the world; yet we have not finished. We are still standing in the middle of our speech. We have no desire to stop, nor are we able to. We refuse to abandon our way of life, our peoplehood, and the spiritual desires that transcend any narrow definition. (SK 1:156)

12

The Holiness of the Body

"We have been so focused on our souls that we have forgotten the holiness of the body."

MANY THINK THAT RELIGION IS FOCUSED SOLELY ON MATTERS of the soul and has little concern for the body. Indeed, some religions even recommend depriving the body as an ideal path toward spiritual purification.

And so too, when Rav Kook made aliyah in 1904, he witnessed two opposing worlds: the religious, absorbed in spiritual matters such as learning Torah and prayer, and the secular Zionists, who were immersed in the physical labor of building the land of Israel.

Yet Rav Kook did not accept this distorted understanding of holiness that perceives the body as the enemy of the soul. When he looked to the heroes of the Tanach, such as Yehoshua, Shimshon, and King David, he found no such dichotomy between spirituality and physicality.

And thus, in this chapter, Rav Kook will introduce us to one of his most important spiritual insights: a return to the land of Israel is a return to appreciating the holiness of the body.

Israel Holiness versus Exile Holiness

Thousands of Years without Physicality

Thousands of years have passed in which our nation has had no involvement in physical matters. We have been a nation floating in the sky. We dreamt only of the kingdom of heaven, of absolute godly goodness. This strange condition acted like a fantastic medicine, for through it we absorbed deep within us the natural yearning for the ideal godly existence.

However, in the present times we are being called back to the physical part of life. This is the *techiyah* (revolution). (O, "Hatechiyah" 3)

Rav Kook was deeply impressed by the secular Zionists working the land (above); he saw this as a revival of the spiritual importance of physicality.

Rav Kook (*center left*) on his fundraising trip in America, 1924.

Heavenly Protest against Detached Spirituality
The more one is connected to spirituality, the more concerned one should be about the world and life in general. In times of destruction, when Jewish strength was separated from its land and was forced to find its purpose only in the realm of detached spirituality, certain individuals were called on to implement a lifestyle of self-denial for the sake of the world to come. Nevertheless, a heavenly protest arose in response to this path.

However, when the time has arrived for building up the nation in its land, and the practical necessities of state and social organization become components of the overall plan, the very physical needs themselves become the essence of Torah. (O, "Hatechiyah" 27)

Holiness versus Nature
The holiness of nature is the holiness of the land of Israel. God's presence that descended into exile with the Jewish People is the ability to establish holiness by opposing nature. But the holiness that fights against nature is not a perfect holiness. It needs to be swallowed up in the deepest truth, in the deepest holiness: the holiness that is found in nature itself, which is the basis for *tikkun olam* (transforming the world). Then the holiness of exile will be connected to the holiness of the land of Israel. "In the future, the synagogues and study houses of Babylon will be established in the land of Israel" (*Megillah* 29a).

When we come to this higher understanding of the perfected holiness of nature, which also comprises the holiness that is above nature and that opposes nature, the battle [between nature and holiness] will cease completely. (O, "Hatechiyah" 28)

The Forgotten Holiness of the Body
The demand for physicality is enormous. We need healthy bodies. But we have been so focused on our souls that we have forgotten the holiness of the body. We have neglected our health and strength, and

have forgotten that we possess holy bodies no less than we possess holy souls. We have abandoned the life of practicality, the training of our senses, and our connection with the concrete material world. All this is due to a lack of faith in holiness of the land of Israel....

All of our *teshuvah* will succeed only if it includes all the glory of holiness. A physical repentance creates healthy blood and mighty bodies. A powerful spirit shines on the strong muscles, and the strength of the holy body will illuminate the weakened soul – this is an allusion to *techiyat hameitim* (the revival of the dead). (O, "Hatechiyah" 33)

Healthy People Do Not Need Medicine

There are times when we see our spiritual leaders focused on self-denial and seclusion. They even frown upon physicality. This is a sign that sickness has come to the world, and in order to be healed from this sickness, they seek the use of extreme medicines that a healthy person does not need. (MaR, p. 235)

Body and Soul in the Land of Israel

In the land of Israel, it is possible to understand that the body of a Jew is holy in exactly the same way that the soul is holy. One does not need to tear the body away from its natural tendencies, but rather to elevate it and feed it with the taste of the holiness of the land of Israel. "The land of Israel makes a person wise" (*Bava Batra* 158b). (SK 3:364)

The Partnership of the Body and Soul

The Harmony of the Body and Soul

The ideal type of faith is when the body and soul are strongly connected; this is the combination of faith based on nature with faith based on tradition. In bringing together the body and the soul, many chambers of light and life are produced.

There are times when these two values are blurred, and the faith of nature and the faith of tradition are separated from each other. As a consequence, an unhealthy version of faith comes about. The greater the separation, the greater the danger.... The healthy version is always harmonious; as the faith of nature grows, the faith of tradition also grows.... Fortunate is the one who always focuses on this ideal goal of combining these two types of faith, the internal and the external. (SK 7:81)

Fixing the Soul through the Body
Sometimes it is only possible to fix a spiritual problem through strengthening the body, and not through *teshuvah* or any other religious act. (SK 1:45)

Teshuvah of the Body
There are some righteous people (*tzaddikim*) whose entire *teshuvah* (spiritual transformation) consists of caring for their bodies. (KYK 2, Pinkas 5:95)

A *Tzaddik* Must Be Physically Strong
Tzaddikim (righteous people) must have powerful and strong bodies so that their good desires will be able to influence the world. The physical weakness of righteous people...weakens the light of the world. (SK 1:44)

Weakness of the Soul Derives from the Body
Sometimes it happens that a person's willpower is weak due to a weakness in the body; the spiritual side of a person is unable to express itself due to a lack of physical strength. In fact, ignoring one's physicality will only increase pain, whereas strengthening the health of one's body would actually strengthen one's spiritual light. This principle is also true concerning an entire people. In regard to the Jewish people, this principle reveals itself at the time of the Mashi-

ach, when there is a demand for physical strength, even though the inner goal is spiritual elevation. (SK 1:426)

The Flaw Is Not Spiritual but Physical
Sometimes one believes oneself to be spiritually wanting and tries to make up for this deficiency, but in the process, falls into even greater deficiencies. This can happen because what was actually lacking was something physical. When what was physically lacking is restored, the spiritual problem will be fixed automatically. This principle is true for an individual as well as an entire nation. (KYK 2, Pinkas 5:70)

The Body Prepares the Ground for the Soul
It is impossible for the soul to have a negative attitude toward the body. This is true even though they have values that seem to contradict....

When we see that people are focusing their efforts on physical and secular goals, that they are immersed in building the nation and the land, and we feel that the essence of life and the source of success rests in more spiritual issues, rather than material building... our hearts should not fall into despair. We should not forget the great importance of preparing the ground for the Soul of all souls. (SK 8:137)

Exercise Can Be Used for Holiness
When the following piece was first published in the book *Orot* in 1921, it met with great opposition from the Old Yishuv. They couldn't accept how much spiritual importance Rav Kook gave to physical exercise.

The exercise that the youth of the Jewish people do in the land of Israel to strengthen their bodies in order to become powerful children of the nation completes the spiritual power of the loftiest righteous people that are immersed in unifying divine names for the sake of increasing light in the world. Indeed, one cannot stand without the other.

Do not be shocked if there are flaws in the lifestyle of those who are involved in strengthening their bodies, or in any material acquirements in the land of Israel, since even the revelation of the spirit of holiness needs cleansing from the remnants of impurity it contains. However, it too improves, purifies, sanctifies, and cleanses. It redeems itself from exile until it comes to the path of righteousness, "a shining light, growing and illuminating until the peak of the day" (Mishlei 4:18). (O, "Hatechiyah" 34)

Judaism Is a Religion of Life, Not Death

The prohibition against a Kohen (priest) coming into contact with a dead body serves to guard us from the extreme attitude of hating life. Since the Kohanim are the teachers of Torah and ethics, one would think that they should be employed at the time of death to instruct the dying in repentance and to soothe the freshly mourning. Indeed, if not for the prohibition, natural feeling would lead to it becoming the custom for a priest to be present at the moment when the soul leaves the body.

Yet this would surely lead the impressionable person to see death as something very glorious and important, and cause the devaluing of life, and eventually hatred for it. But "the Torah of God is perfect" (Tehillim 19:8), and it is called "the Torah of life," and the lessons that come from it through the mouths of the leaders must also be connected with life. The Torah therefore distances the priest, who has the job of teaching the practical and spiritual laws of God, from these types of services. This protects the general ethics, which are easily affected by the leaders, from the extreme ideas that tend to develop in relation to the unknown. As it is written, "Do not be overly righteous, nor be overly wise; why destroy yourself?" (Kohelet 7:16). (KYK 1, Pinkas Acharon b'Boisk 2)

Sacrifice the Law, Not the Body
Letter to the Labor Center and the Maccabi Health Clinic (both involved in the financial and health concerns of people in Israel), August 28, 1913

Rav Kook wrote the following letter in response to the terrible misrepresentation of the Torah seen in an incident in which a young boy was turned away from the hospital on Shabbat due to certain religious people's fear that he wasn't quite sick enough to operate on. As a consequence, the boy tragically passed away.

My soul is full of sadness and brokenheartedness over the tragic event of this young boy.... There is absolutely no way I can believe that any Jew with the most basic *reiach shel Torah* (sense of Torah) would not know the simplest *halachah* about the importance of breaking Shabbat for the sake of *pikuach nefesh* (saving someone's life). Even if a person has a doubt of a doubt of a doubt, one should still break Shabbat.... Because the ancient rabbis have already taught us that "Shabbat was given for the sake of the Jewish people, and the Jewish people were not given for the sake of Shabbat" (*Yoma* 85b). (IR 2, pp. 212–13)

Don't Try to Outsmart Your Body
One will never succeed in the effort to convert one's body into spirit, in the effort to create for the body a new and unsuitable nature. The same deficiencies that appear primitive and wild when viewed from the perspective of the soul are, when found in the body, like the salt that gives everything flavor, and the wine that is produced from fermentation.

Therefore, one should not try to outsmart one's animal instincts, even though at first glance they seem like the enemy of the soul. Rather, one should ascend to the heights of wisdom, the light of knowledge, and learn from the principles of Torah to channel the valuable parts of physicality. And in due time, the sickness of the body will be healed. (SK 5:274)

Stop Ignoring Your Body

A letter to Rabbi Yaakov Moshe Charlap (one of Rav Kook's closest students, who served as the *rosh yeshiva* of Mercaz HaRav), September 25, 1908 (Erev Rosh Hashanah)

> ...For God's sake, your spiritual growth should only be done with joy, without any type of sadness and anxiety.... Do not do anything that will damage your health. Doing this is merely your *yetzer hara*. Instead, you must give your body rest and relaxation. Better is one hour of Torah and prayer in a peaceful and loving state of mind than many days of devotion in an atmosphere of sadness. (IR 1, p. 92)

My Evil Inclination Is Telling Me to Fast

> Dr. Falk Schlesinger was Rav Kook's physician in the last days of his life. He recalled how Rav Kook consulted with him shortly before Tisha b'Av – at the height of his illness – about whether or not he should fast. Rav Kook said, "My *yetzer hara* (evil inclination) tells me to fast, while my *yetzer tov* (good inclination) tells me not to." (Simcha Raz, *An Angel among Men*, p. 450)

The Third Song
The Song of Humanity

13

Faith and Science

"In our generation, we must explain all matters of faith, Torah, and religious acts in an intelligent way."

IN THE MINDS OF MANY PEOPLE, RELIGION COMMUNICATES divine truth, while science conveys human truth. And therefore, when a scientific theory seems to contradict the Torah, it is expected that a religious person will reject science in favor of godly wisdom.

For example, when the Torah says that the world was created in six days, and modern science contradicts this through the theory of evolution, is a religious person not obligated to reject evolution and continue to stubbornly believe in the six days of creation?

The seemingly contradictory relationship between faith and science has been a topic of frustration for spiritual seekers throughout the world for many years.

Yet, according to Rav Kook, the problem of faith and science does not come from any fundamental contradiction between divine and human truth, but rather, from a misunderstanding of the purpose of the Torah.

In this chapter, Rav Kook will explain to us how faith relates to science, and what the Torah is really trying to teach us.

Faith Is Not Irrational

Explaining Faith Intelligently
In our generation, we must explain all matters of faith, Torah, and religious acts in an intelligent way. (SK 1:215)

When "Fear of God" Is "Fear of Thinking"
The greatest danger of having *yirat shamayim* (fear of God) is when it isn't clearly connected to the light of Torah. *Yirat hachet* (fear of sin) becomes confused and turns into *yirat hamachshavah* (fear of thinking). When a person becomes afraid of thinking, he slowly starts drowning in the swamp of ignorance. It removes the light of one's soul, weakens one's strength, and clouds one's spirit. (OK 3 p. 26)

Secular Knowledge Is Important
A letter to Rabbi Yitzchak Levi (secretary and cofounder of Yeshivat Merkaz HaRav), February 4, 1908

The great rabbis of the land of Israel, who include many authentic scholars and *tzaddikim*, have prohibited the study of any secular wisdom and foreign languages. In fact, they have not even permitted the learning of the official language of the state. Yet this prohibition has become like a copper chain on the necks of people who fear God and walk in the path of purity. These religious people have no practical path toward educating their children. They are beginning to see with their own eyes that it is impossible to survive in the modern era without the tools of a modern language and basic knowledge.

On the other hand, secular Jews, who have abandoned the life of Torah and mitzvot, are educating their children in schools that give expert training and preparation for the problems of life. Sadly, it is only the children of parents who are connected to the holy Torah and the belief in God who are left unprepared on the path of life.

Therefore, since arriving here in Israel, I, small and unimportant, have expressed my opinion to a small number of holy rabbis that it is unhealthy for this path of life to continue any longer. "We must anticipate what the future will bring" (*Pirkei Avot* 2:9) and "prepare the medicine before the sickness" (*Megillah* 13b). I have already expressed my opinion that we are currently in a situation of "a time to act for God, to put aside the Torah" (Tehillim 119:126). We must introduce dramatic changes to the curriculum of our children, who have been educated only with Torah and mitzvot. They must be given the necessary tools of language and knowledge in order to confront the trials of life. (IR 1, p. 139)

Must the Torah Be Read Literally?

A letter to Rabbi Dr. Moshe Seidel (professor of Bible studies at the Rabbi Isaac Elchanan Theological Seminary and one of Rav Kook's closest students), May 6, 1908

I feel an inner obligation to explain to your pure soul how to deal with the many new scientific opinions that contradict the literal words of the Torah. My opinion is that any person who has an honest mind must understand that even though these new scientific truths are not absolutely proven, nevertheless, we certainly do not have any obligation to deny and reject them. Indeed, it is definitely not one of the goals of the Torah to simply tell facts and historical episodes. Instead, the main goal is the philosophical principles, the inner spiritual meaning. And thus, whenever there is an area in the Torah that contradicts science, we must always search for the deeper meaning of the text in order to overcome the problem.

This principle of interpretation was already taught in the words of the sages (Rishonim), and specifically in the Rambam's *Guide for the Perplexed*. In today's age, we must be willing to expand and apply their words even further.

It does not matter whether there once existed a paradise where mankind enjoyed overflowing physical and spiritual pleasures or whether existence evolved from the lowest to the highest... and is still evolving until this day.

The only thing that we must know for certain is that it is possible for a person to rise to the highest heights... and in spite of all this, if one becomes corrupted, it is possible to lose everything. In fact, one is able to do damage to both oneself as well as several generations to follow. This is the main lesson that we learn from the existence of man in the Garden of Eden, his sin and his being expelled.

This is a very important principle when it comes to conflicting opinions: when there is an opinion that contradicts something in the Torah, to begin with, we must not immediately refute it; rather, we must build the castle of the Torah on top of this opinion. And by doing this, we are able to rise by way of the opposing opinion, and because of this, further understanding is revealed. And then, since we have removed the pressure, we will also be able to disagree with the opinion in perfect faith, if necessary. (IR 1, pp. 163–64)

The Theory of Evolution

Evolution Fits the Teachings of Kabbalah

The theory of evolution that is currently spreading and conquering the world fits with the kabbalistic understanding of the world, much more than any other scientific or philosophical theory. The theory of evolution, which believes in a pathway of constant development, creates an essentially optimistic understanding of the world. Indeed, how can a person despair when one sees that everything is evolving and ascending?

In fact, when we penetrate into the depths of the theory of evolution, we discover an element of the Divine, shining in complete clarity – that it is specifically the actualized aspect of the Divine that is causing the potential aspect of the Divine to become materialized.

Evolution expresses its light on all the ways of the Divine. All of existence is evolving and ascending. And just as this is apparent in the parts of existence, it is in fact true of the whole as well. Eventually it will evolve toward the greatest good, where no detail will be left out, and no spark will be lost. (OK 2 p. 537)

Heretics Help Uncover Divine Truth

In all areas of the Torah that heretics criticize and throw away lie the very answers to their questions and objections. This is true both with regard to criticism of words and letters of the Torah as well as spiritual and intellectual characteristics. All those arguments and paths that led to heresy bring one to a deeper and more elevated understanding of faith once one uncovers their deeper source. Indeed, one's faith becomes more enlightened and healthy than the simplistic faith that preceded it. Furthermore, it is evolution, which naturally and logically develops from small to big, from the lowest creation to the highest... that teaches us about the ultimate goal of existence.

It is through evolution that divine greatness is glorified. In fact, all of the goals of faith become confirmed, and the significance of belief, trust, and service of God expand. Because everything is evolving toward a greater goal... when humans develop themselves and the world around them... they are really doing the will of God. (OK 2, p. 548)

Science Does Not Contradict the Torah

LAZY THINKING CREATES MISUNDERSTANDINGS

A letter to Rabbi Dr. Moshe Seidel (professor of Bible studies at the Rabbi Isaac Elchanan Theological Seminary and one of Rav Kook's closest students), June 13, 1905

I have received your pleasant letter. If I had more time, it would have been appropriate to reply to you in depth, to explain the root of each subject that you wrote about, to address all the important issues that arise in regard to science and faith. Indeed, all mistakes come about only because a person doesn't search and investigate;

one tries to solve the most serious problems using simplistic thinking. As a consequence, the truth becomes distorted. Therefore, it is our obligation to clarify matters of truth from the Torah of truth.

KABBALISTIC SOLUTION

Concerning the age of the world according to modern geological calculations: According to all kabbalistic opinions, there existed many time periods before what we mark as the beginning of the world. Even according to the Midrash, "God built many worlds and destroyed many worlds" (*Bereishit Rabbah* 70:3). And according to the *Zohar*, there were many species of people besides Adam, who is written about in the Torah (*Zohar*, Vayikra, p. 10).

Therefore, those opinions teach us that there did indeed exist many time periods before the one we began dating – the period of modern humanity being just one of them.

AN EVEN EASIER SOLUTION

But in truth, we do not even need these kabbalistic solutions. Indeed, even if it became clear to us that the order of creation came about through the evolution of species, there is still no problem with us counting the years of creation according to the literal words of the Torah....

It is well known that the Torah purposely spoke vaguely regarding the creation of the world, and communicated itself in hints and metaphors. It is understood that the Torah's description of the creation of the world is a part of the mystical section of the Torah. If the description of the creation of the world was supposed to be taken completely literally, how could it contain mystical secrets?

The Midrash says, "It is impossible to explain the power of the creation of the world. Therefore, the Torah simply wrote, 'God created the world'" (*Guide for the Perplexed*, introduction; Ramban, Bereishit 1). The most important thing about the story is the understanding one gains about God, and about living a truly moral life.

SCIENTIFIC THEORIES ARE ALWAYS EVOLVING

There is never a contradiction between any part of the Torah and science. Nevertheless, a theory is not necessarily a fact, even if it is well accepted. Scientific theories are like unripe fruit that constantly evolves. All the most modern theories will one day be laughed at, and all the most sophisticated wisdom of our generation will be understood as immature thoughts. Only the word of God will last forever. "'Though the mountains will fall and the hills will collapse, yet My unfailing love for you will not fall, nor will my covenant of peace collapse,' says God, Who has compassion for you" (Yeshayahu 54:10).

CREATION DOESN'T PRECLUDE NATURAL PROCESS

The essence of what we are saying is that everything is God's creation, and the steps of the process – be they many or only a few – are all actions of God. Now, sometimes the Torah will describe in detail the different steps of the process, and sometimes the Torah will simply skip the steps and say, "God created," "God acted." This is similar to how the Torah says, "And King Solomon created"; here we do not need to be told that King Solomon commanded the officers, and the officers commanded those lower officers, and the architects the artists, and the artists the builders. In this example, it is obvious what we mean, and also, the details are not of essential importance.

In fact, even if we were to investigate over thousands of years all the intricacies of the process, although this would certainly give us wisdom and knowledge of the greatness of the Divine, nevertheless, these descriptions would still be limited and unable to fully explain what occurred.

SCIENTIFIC KNOWLEDGE REVEALS ITSELF SLOWLY

In truth, there is a reason that every idea and thought comes to the world at a specific time period. Nothing is random and unintended. For example, we can comprehend that if people came to know thousands of years too early that the earth is constantly revolving, they might have been afraid to stand up, lest they fall off the planet. All the more so would they have feared to build tall buildings. This knowledge would have accordingly impeded normal development. The calculations of gravity would not have comforted them, since their own experience showed them much more tangibly that anything standing atop a moving object is in danger of toppling off.

Only after many years of maturing the mind was humanity in a healthy enough mindset to uncover the wisdom of the earth's movement, for the good of all people.

HAVE CONFIDENCE IN YOURSELF
When you understand what I have said, you will recognize that there is great worth to both the literal meaning of the Torah as well as the hidden meaning of the Torah. Indeed, there are many wondrous ways of hidden meaning and paths of divine wisdom.... And when you walk in this path, you can be certain that with God's help you will not make a mistake.

"I will lead the blind by ways they have not known, along unfamiliar paths I will guide them; I will turn the darkness into light before them and make the rough places smooth. These are the things I will do; I will not forsake them" (Yeshayahu 42:16). (IR 1, pp. 105–7)

Evolution Should Bring Knowledge of God

The Rambam already wrote that the stories of creation told in the Torah should not be understood literally; rather, they have a deeper lesson to teach. In fact, the Rambam said that if he had an absolute proof of the eternity of the world, then he would interpret the verses of creation in the same metaphorical way that he explained verses with human descriptions of God.

Now, it is clear and obvious that the modern theory of evolution does not contradict the main foundations of the Torah at all – not even the verses describing the creation of the world. A person may however try to argue that if, for example, just the material of the planet took tens of thousands of years to form, then we don't see any godly involvement. Why should creation need to take so much time? Why was it not instant?

To these questions, we can reply that the world evolving step by step does not at all keep us from a recognition of God. It in fact brings the soul close to God in deep love and upliftment. When we look at the many forces of the world, and we see how everything is organized in perfect order, with great wisdom, kindness, and compassion, we recognize the sustaining force of all, which is the living God.

And what is the difference between the evolution of the stars and constellations over tens of thousands of years, and the evolution of the fetus in the womb of a mother over many months? Concerning the baby, we still recognize that "Your creations are incredible; my soul knows this very well.... When I was made in a secret place, when I was woven together in the depths of the earth, Your eyes saw my unformed body; everything was written in Your book" (Tehillim 139:14–16).

All the more so should we be amazed if we examine the order of evolution from the simplest organisms up to the intelligence, righteousness, honesty, and power of a human being. (PR 2, pp. 25–26)

14

Liberal and Progressive Values

"The highest type of thinking... never rejects any idea in the world. Instead, it purifies it and guides it toward the good."

AS THE WORLD CHANGES, MORAL VALUES CHANGE WITH IT. WHILE in the past it may have been common to excommunicate a person who had atheistic beliefs, today this is considered extreme and counterproductive. Once, preventing a woman from having a public position was the norm; today it is called sexist. Previously, hunting animals for sport was celebrated as a gentleman's hobby; today, hunting for sport is frowned upon by many. In the past, persecuting and criticizing a person because of religious beliefs that differed from those of the majority was standard; today it is considered bigotry and intolerance.

While many will agree that as history changes, morals change with it, the question of whether religion changes with the times is greatly debated. If religion is eternally true, does that not imply that its values should never change? And if religion does change with the times, does that not uproot its authority?

In this chapter, Rav Kook will explore the complex issue of how religion must address liberal and progressive values.

Searching for Divine Truth in Liberal Values

How One Uses an Object

The less sophisticated one is, the less capable one is of distinguishing between people or objects and the conduct of these people or objects. Most people, in order to improve themselves, are forced to prepare for the road toward goodness by establishing a worldview based on a hatred of evil. This hatred of evil is unable to differentiate between the actual evil and the people who do evil – but after all, "the Torah was not given to angels" (*Kiddushin* 54a, *Sotah* 33a, *Me'ilah* 14b, etc.). Even though this is destructive, since by hating the possessor of evil one hates the good within him too, the general character of man is such that this is the way it must be.

However, the ideal trait of powerful souls is the ability to clarify and distinguish. Their hatred of evil is "clean," directed only at the evil object itself. Because it is properly directed, this negative feeling brings them to the positive feeling of the love of good, and thus the light of kindness shines in the glory of their wisdom. (OK 4, p. 497)

Fear versus Caution

Fear is unsophisticated. In truth, a person need not fear anything. One is only required to show caution. The more one fears, the more one stumbles, and the fear of fear itself makes this even worse. Therefore, one must be firm in one's mind that there is nothing to fear at all. (MR, "Pachdanut" 4)

Searching for the Good

How does one elevate the sparks of holiness from the depths of evil?

One must first purify the heart through logical, refined musar (self-improvement). Then, one must sanctify the heart through lofty thoughts of inner connection and knowledge of God. Finally, one must probe the expansive thoughts that encompass all the realms of one's soul, and all the concepts that drift throughout the world, and begin to distinguish in all of them between the good and the bad. One must be meticulous in examining even concepts that wicked people have used for evil, to discern whether there might indeed be some spark of good in them.

When one discovers a spark of good from the depths of evil, one must strengthen it, purify it, expand it, and uncover what one can practically take from it. (SK 1:78)

How to Approach Those Who Oppose Us

A letter to Rabbi Milstein (a *shochet* who was a great admirer of Rav Kook), in response to a letter from Rabbi Milstein asking Rav Kook for advice concerning his sons who had abandoned religion, January 16, 1907

My way is to relate to the youth with the trait of absolute kindness and to explain to them how many good points exist within their ideals. Their entire mistake is that what they think is good, they feel is opposite to the Torah; but in truth, it is the essence of the Torah. (IR 1, p. 58)

Pessimistic Religion Is Destroying Us

A letter to Rabbi Elazar Baichowsky (a Chabad rabbi), April 23, 1908

Our collapse has come about not because rabbis do not protest against the institutions of atheists that are destroying the holy land, but because they only protest, and nothing else. We are being forced to admit that even Chasidut, which was meant to reveal the divine light in every heart and mind, has changed its character. Today it is heading only in the path of an unsophisticated fear. Indeed, there is very little difference between the Chasidim and the Mitnagdim. (IR 1, p. 160)

Spirituality That Focuses on Positivity
We need to develop a spiritual outlook that will not focus on the negativities in secular values, but instead concentrate on transforming them into a more spiritual and beautiful form. (SK 6:230)

The Personality of a *Tzaddik*
The purest *tzaddikim* (righteous individuals) do not complain about evil, but instead increase righteousness. They do not complain about atheism, but instead increase faith. They do not complain about ignorance, but instead increase wisdom. (AT 80)

The Teaching of the Mashiach
When the light of the Mashiach illuminates one's heart, it will teach one to give respect to all creatures. (SK 1:891)

Finding a Spark of Truth in Everything
We must continually find the spark of truth in everything. Only then will the light of the world be revealed in its highest form. (SK 1:890)

How to Overcome Negativity
It is only possible to overcome the negativity that we find in the world or in the Jewish people by uncovering the elements of truth contained within them and redirecting them to a good and holy path. (SK 1:216)

Never Reject an Idea
The highest type of thinking...never rejects any idea in the world. Instead, it purifies it and guides it toward the good. (SK 1:480)

Progress through Imperfection
It is impossible to demand, from oneself or from the world, ideals that are totally pure and without some mixture of the dirt that comes from the base nature of the individual and society. The main princi-

ple of successful progress is that a person should always be involved in Torah and mitzvot even for non-ideal motives; because from non-ideal motivations, one will eventually come to ideal motivations (a paraphrase from *Sanhedrin* 105b). (SK 8:68)

Perfecting Imperfect Ideas

There are important ideas that, when fully completed, become the source of all matters of goodness and holiness. Yet when these ideas are left incomplete, they have many negative consequences. This is also true when it comes to important people who made mistakes and caused a stumbling block for others. It is possible for even greater people to come after them and to take the thoughts of these people and complete them so that they can guide them to a holy and ethical goal. (KYK 1, Pinkas Rishon l'Yaffo 3)

Belief in God Is the Opposite of Dogma

Godliness has the virtue of a singular idea, yet it does not lack the benefits of infinite ideas. And anyone who thinks that the thought of God is like a burden – since it seems to be dogmatic, set in a single view – has not even begun to enter into the inner depths of the Divine. (KYK 2, Pinkas 5:10)

Rav Kook on his way to the White House in 1924

History Reveals God

The Evolution of Liberalism

When this essay was originally published in OK 2, pp. 544–46, it was censored, and the word *anarchy* was taken out of the fourth paragraph. Due to the recent publication of the original diary entries, I have translated it and put it back into the essay.

UNCIVILIZED MAN VERSUS CIVILIZED MAN

The world is made up of a goodness that constantly increases, and it is this same goodness that is also revealed in the desire and nature of humankind. In the past, man's nature and desires were coarser than they are now, and in the future they will be more refined than they are at present. In the past, the core of Torah and musar was directed more toward nullifying natural desire, because it was overflowing with evil. In the future it will develop and take on a new form, to the point that the expression of man's innate desires in all of their capacity will become a moral necessity, and it will then be evident how much good is embodied within them.

CONSERVATIVES VERSUS LIBERALS

However, in the present state, man's desires still have many unrefined elements, and because of the merit of the good parts, the dregs also rise and become free – and in their freedom, they contaminate the world and destroy it. This creates a heated war, and each camp defends with honesty and fights with honesty. The liberals fight on behalf of the good elements of the will, in order that they not suffer unnecessary restraint, which is only detrimental. The conservatives, who know the past and understand its glorious good, defend the restrictions, in order that the corrupt elements of the will not destroy the moral principles of the world. The great souls must be peacekeepers between the fighters of this war by showing each side the proper boundary that is truly appropriate for it.

HOW DID LIBERALISM EVOLVE?

In the ancient days, the collective intelligence of mankind was less advanced, and its desires were more barbaric. Consequently, the divine vision was entirely directed toward pushing away the rebellious intellect that was enslaved to the animalistic desires of human society. It continually pushed away the natural desire that was more inspired by encounters with filth and sin. The world eventually became well grounded after a period of many generations, through the revelation of the Divine Presence within the Jewish people (giving of the Torah), challenges and experiences throughout history, improvement in social relationships (globalization), and the advancement of science and wisdom. All these helped to refine the spirit of man. Even though it has not yet completely refined him, a large portion of his intelligence and natural desires has become directed on its own to the godly good.

HOW WE MUST APPROACH THIS WAR

Corresponding to the degree to which it has already been refined, liberalism is certain to spread, and anarchy will find its place. And when tradition and religion come, even in their most sophisticated form, to conquer this refined portion, they will not succeed. Instead, religion needs to encourage the spirit of man in the refined elements that it has already reached, and to refocus its attention toward those elements of the spirit, intelligence, and desire of mankind that are yet to be grounded, and are still standing in their state of corruption, like in ancient days.

IS LIBERALISM DANGEROUS?

The danger in the excitement over the refined elements is when the corrupt parts, the leftover barbaric elements, are given room to move in their natural wild state, and the part of man that is refined covers over them with wings of delusion, to spread a shiny covering over all the filth and lies.

The Work of Spiritual Souls
This is the holy work of spiritual souls until the end of days, until the spirit of impurity totally disappears, and the beauty of man and the world will be revealed in its proper balance in the Kingdom of God. (SK 1:109)

The Masses Are Getting Smarter
In the earlier generations, most people were not very intelligent. At the same time, the geniuses were giants in knowledge, so that they could be capable of lifting up the undeveloped masses. Yet as history progressed, knowledge expanded to the masses, and the geniuses became less great.

This is because God desires the perfection of humanity; and since perfection comes about through the balance of strengths, when the masses are deficient, the intelligent minority will be far above them. Thus, the more the masses develop, the more the geniuses become closer to average. This will happen until all the masses rise up to such a level that "no longer will they teach their neighbor, or say to one another, 'Know God,' because they will all know Me, from the least of them to the greatest" (Yirmiyahu 31:34). (KYK 1, Pinkas Rishon l'Yaffo 79)

This Generation Is Not a Low Generation
The present generation is not a low generation, but rather a very high and superior one. It is unable to walk in the lesser path of habit because it desires to understand and know. We must give it wisdom, and welcome it with an optimistic attitude. Its values of righteousness and ethics are extremely idealistic, and we only need to purify and elevate them. (KYK 1, Pinkas Rishon l'Yaffo 130)

Transformation of the Old and New
A letter to Rabbi Dr. Moshe Seidel (professor of Bible studies at the Rabbi Isaac Elchanan Theological Seminary and one of Rav Kook's closest students), October 21, 1908

We must not turn our backs on the old, but use the new to understand the inner wisdom of the old. We must begin to recognize how the new can combine with the old and transform it. The old will become new, and the new will become holy [*hayashan yitchadesh, v'hachadash yitkadesh*]. (IR 1, p. 214)

The Holy Rebel

TWO TYPES OF SOULS

The respected way of living, based on justice, the requisites of good character, and conformity to law, corresponds to the way of the *olam hatikkun* (world of order). Every rebellion against this, whether inspired by superficial inspiration or by the stirring of a higher spirit, reflects the *olam hatohu* (world of chaos). But there is a vast difference in the particular expressions of the *olam hatohu*. The great idealists seek an order so noble, so firm and pure, beyond what may be found in the world of reality, and thus they destroy what has been fashioned in conformity to the norms of the world. The best among them also know how to rebuild the world that has been thus destroyed, but those of lesser stature, who have been touched only slightly by the inclination to idealism, are only destroyers, and they are rooted in the *olam hatohu* on its lowest level.

THE *OLAM HATOHU* SOUL

The souls inspired by the *olam hatohu* (world of chaos) are greater than the souls of the *olam hatikkun* (world of order). They are very great; they demand so much from reality, even that which is beyond their own ability to endure. They cannot bear what is limited, whatever is confined within a prescribed measure. Their endless striving knows no bounds. They robe themselves in various forms, aspiring constantly to what is beyond the measure of the possible. They aspire and they fall, realizing that they are confined in rules, in limiting conditions that forbid expansion toward the unlimited horizons, and they fall in sorrow, in despair, in anger – and anger leads to wickedness, defiance, destruction, and every other evil.

The souls inspired by a destructive passion reveal themselves especially at the end of days, before the great disaster that precedes the emergence of a new and more wondrous level of existence. In times of redemption, chutzpah is ever increasing. A fierce storm rages, more breaches appear, and acts of chutzpah grow continuously because no satisfaction can be found in the solutions offered by a limited light. It does not satisfy all the yearnings of these souls, nor does it unravel for them the mystery of existence. They rebel against everything, including the dimension of the good that could lead them to a great peace and help them rise to great heights. They rebel and they are outraged, they break and they discard. They seek their nourishment in alien pastures, embracing foreign ideals and desecrating everything sacred, but without finding peace.

OLAM HATOHU FRIGHTENS OLAM HATIKKUN
These passionate souls express their strength so powerfully that no fence can hold them back. The weaklings of the *olam hatikkun* (established order), who are guided by balance and normalcy, are too terrified to tolerate them. The feeling of these souls of *olam hatikkun* is expressed in Yeshayahu (33:14): "Who among us can dwell with this devouring fire? Who among us can dwell with those who destroy the world?"

TZADDIKIM ARE NOT FRIGHTENED
But in truth, there is no need to be terrified. Only sinners, the weak in spirit, and hypocrites are frightened and seized by terror. Truly noble spirits know that this force is one of the phenomena needed for the perfection of the world, for strengthening the power of the nation and humanity. Although this force is initially expressed in chaos, in the end it will be taken from the wicked and turned over to the hands of the righteous, who will show the truth about perfection and construction with great courage, inspired by clear perception and a steady and undimmed sense of the practical. (O, "Zeronim" 3)

The Evolution of Optimistic Religion

Up until the redemption, we have only taught the world a divine wisdom of obligations and moral restrictions. But people do not like obligations, and when they accept them anyway, a grudge lingers in their hearts concerning whoever is responsible for them. For ethics truly come to restrict and imprison our animalistic passions. But when the *geulah* (the time period of revealing light to the world) has arrived, it will be made known that what we are giving is a path to true pleasure – a happiness that gives life value, and without which, all fades away.

Since pleasure and happiness are attractive to everyone, those responsible for discovering this will be honored and respected. As it is written, "Ten people from all the different nations will grab on to the fringes of each Jewish person" (Zechariah 8:23). (O, "Yisrael" 5.15)

15

Relationship to Other Religions

"God performed an act of kindness for His world in not putting all talent and wisdom in one place: not in one person, not in one nation, not in one land, not in one generation, and not even in one world. Instead, all talent and wisdom is scattered and spread about."

MANY RELIGIOUS WARS THROUGHOUT HISTORY HAVE BEEN fought based on the assumption that if a person's religious beliefs are true, then any other religious beliefs must be false. There have even been wars fought within a single religion because of differences in the interpretation of that particular faith. Indeed, there is a great danger when people believe that one religion contains all truth, while the rest are totally false.

Rav Kook couldn't accept this dogmatic attitude toward truth; he didn't think that Judaism asked one to believe that one people or person contains all truth. On the other hand, he also understood that there is a major danger in religious pluralism; for if truth exists in all religions, then why should a person follow any specific religion?

This is the main dilemma when dealing with tolerance and interfaith relationships: How does one remain loyal to one's own faith while also respecting and recognizing truth in other religions?

In this chapter, Rav Kook will show us how to be dedicated to one's own tradition while being open to the wisdom within all traditions.

Truth within Other Religions

No One Has a Monopoly on Truth
God performed an act of kindness for His world in not putting all talent and wisdom in one place: not in one person, not in one nation, not in one land, not in one generation, and not even in one world. Instead, all talent and wisdom is scattered and spread about.

Therefore, in order to reach universal perfection, which is man's most idealistic aspiration, we are forced to seek ultimate peace and unity. While the treasure of wisdom is secretly buried within the Jewish people, in order to unify the entire world together with it, the nation must be flawed and deficient in certain wisdoms. Therefore, the Jewish people must be open to being influenced. (O, "Yisrael" 5:2.3)

There Is Truth in Other Religions
There are unquestionably many things that were said in the Torah – whether mitzvot or stories – that can be found in the words of the greatest spiritual leaders of the ancient non-Jewish nations. The godly wisdom of Moshe was in his ability to transform and purify these ideas from their deficiencies. The more these actions and stories became valuable to life and study, the more they encapsulated God's will.

From this we can learn that the Jewish people cannot be praised for creating and introducing the laws of morality and ethics to the world; not even for creating the source of God's unity. On the contrary, the seven Noahide laws were already passed down from Adam to Noach, and expanded through the teachings of Avraham, his descendants, and many other righteous of the generation.

What the Jewish people can be praised for is building and developing these good teachings. Certainly, this role should not be considered less important just because the Jewish people weren't the original source. On the contrary, the power of truth – which is the real inheritance of the Jewish people – is even more significant when we realize that its origins can be found in all types of people who contain the divine image. God created humanity with truth, and only with the distortion of truth was it necessary for a nation to take on the role of building and upholding truth for the world.

And therefore, there are definitely many good things that can be found among ancient non-Jewish prophets and their followers. In the earliest books of the non-Jewish nations, one can find many wise character traits, actions, knowledge, and stories, even things that are very similar to those in the Torah.

Certainly, there always existed very spiritual individuals among the non-Jews who discovered, through their own natural intelligence, some of the value of the mitzvot. Nevertheless, these mitzvot were only given their full divine expression through the Torah and its eternal covenant with the Jewish people. It was through the combination of prophecy with these ancient wisdoms that they were transformed into divine laws and teachings.

Therefore … it should strengthen our faith and awareness of God when we find among the ancient non-Jewish nations things that are similar to the Torah. Just as we are able to uncover intelligent explanations of the Torah, so too are we able to discover non-Jewish sources that are similar to the Torah, because of the natural ability of humanity to grasp truth on its own. (PR 2, pp. 113–14)

Do Not Be Disrespectful

A letter to Rabbi Aaron Simcha Blumenthal (author of many books, including a pamphlet called *The Religion of Israel*, which Rav Kook criticizes for being unnecessarily negative toward other religions), July 3, 1913

It is wrong to teach about the spiritual greatness of the Jewish people by making disrespectful and condescending remarks about other religions – no matter what they are. Instead, what we need to do is simply focus on the unique and holy qualities of the Torah, and the necessary critiques will be self-evident. (IR 2, p. 199)

Love of All Nations
Love of humanity must be alive in one's heart and soul – a love of each human being as well as a love of all nations, with a desire for both their physical and spiritual transformation. One's hatred must only be focused on those elements of evil and impurity that exist in the world. It is impossible for a person to come to the higher spiritual awareness of "Acknowledge God, and call out in His name; inform the nations of His actions" (I Divrei Hayamim 16:8) without an inner love, stemming from the depths of one's heart and soul: a desire to help all nations, to improve their material lives, and to bring them joy. This personality trait prepares the spirit of the Mashiach to come to the Jewish people.

In any place (in the Torah or Gemara) that we find references to hatred, we must recognize that the real intention is focused on the evil inside.... But we must remember that the essence of life and light can never be removed from the image of God that each human being and nation has been given. (SK 1:807)

Truth within Christianity

The Holy Motivation of Christianity
Sometimes the overemphasis of details, even in matters of holiness and the performance of mitzvot, can damage authentic piety and perfection. There are no lies that do not include a spark of truth. However, as long as the element of truth is not clearly explained, the power of lies begins to spread over everything.

The opposition against laws found its voice through a certain school of thought, which little by little drifted away and eventually abandoned its nation and God. Over a long period of time, these sinners grew in number, due to many racial, social, and economic factors, until soon enough a potent hatred of the Jewish people had planted itself on firm foundations. Nevertheless, the deeper motivation that this was all built upon was a hatred of law.

This group is of course Christianity. However, this poison of hating laws continued to spread. It became a stumbling block for sophisticated individuals of our own people, and sometimes even for simpletons. In our generation, it has reached its peak, whereby our youth, who themselves do not know where this inner hatred comes from, are being infected with this ancient sickness.

WHY WAS CHRISTIANITY SO SUCCESSFUL?

The reason that this hatred of laws succeeded in spreading throughout the universal soul is due to a spark of truth that is hidden deep within it. When the law grows and expands in its many branches and details while the development of its inner content and source (its divine truths and lofty morals) is abandoned, it weakens the soul and dries up all of life. It begins to create an exaggerated fear and trembling, and those who perform it have no peace. Even pious individuals feel the sap of life being sucked out of them and the law strangling them.

WHAT CAN WE LEARN FROM CHRISTIANITY?

Now, in order to stop this path from growing, a power of hating laws was planted. This hatred of divine laws found its voice within the Jewish people itself. Those haters of the law feel within their souls a deep contradiction. However, since they do not fully understand where it is coming from, they lack the means to solve it. Usually the most sensitive, poetic, and spiritual souls are those who feel this sickness most. They begin to look at the law from a point of view of alienation and fear.

In order to treat this sickness at its root, we must begin to strengthen and develop the inner depths of the Torah by learning *aggadah*, Jewish philosophy, and kabbalah. Only then will each mitzvah and each small detail reveal a wealth of depth. With this knowledge, the more one is careful with the Torah's details, the more one will discover the most profound truths. (MaR, p. 288)

Christianity Abandoned Its Jewish Roots

The desire for independence, for the shining spirituality of ancient days, was sometimes strongly felt within the Jewish people. At times, inspirational souls rose up and attempted to return the nation to its youthfulness through charismatic individuality... in order that the Torah would be based on the spiritual revelation of existence.... But these people were not always successful.

During such a vulnerable period, Christianity came and split the nation into pieces. Its main force was a very charismatic personality with a deep sense of spirituality. Unfortunately, it couldn't escape the flaw of idolatry. It increased spirituality at the expense of ethical and educational training. People were so drawn to this person's spiritual personality, and became so obsessed with him, that they eventually abandoned his Jewish characteristics. Their actions and spirit soon became rooted in another source of life. (MaR, pp. 5–6)

Complimenting Jesus

A letter to Rabbi Milstein (a *shochet* who was a great admirer of Rav Kook), August 13, 1911

Regarding your question about that which I wrote concerning "Oto Ha'ish" [Jesus], that he had a "charismatic personality with a deep sense of spirituality," and how there were certain individuals who were shocked by my writing this...

My dear friend, in the current period we are living in, when many of our people have been convinced to leave our religion, I have seen it as my holy obligation to explain these matters.

In truth, this was always the way of the wise men of the Jewish people – not to diminish the personality of the great wicked men, but instead, to demonstrate their enormous potential, and how despite all of this, they fell into destruction and impurity. As it is written concerning Bilam, "In the Jewish people there has never risen a prophet like Moshe, but among the gentiles there was one – this is Bilam" (Sifri).

Only the small-minded are angry with me; the authentic *talmidei chachamim* (wise Torah scholars), who understand the secrets of God, will perceive the benefits of my words. These matters are *razei Torah* (secrets of the Torah), and because of this great time of need, I have decided to reveal them. Greater minds than mine have suffered from the complaints of our people due to matters similar to this. It was an inner drive in their souls that pushed them to reveal profound wisdom for the purpose of *tikkun hador* (fixing the generation). (IR 2, p. 33)

The Fourth Song
The Song of Creation

16

Animal Rights and Vegetarianism

"Surely it is impossible to imagine that the Master of all beings, Who 'has compassion on His creatures' (Tehillim 145:9), would create an eternal law within His creation, which is called 'very good' (Bereishit 1:31), that makes it impossible for humankind to survive without distorting its moral sensitivity by murdering animals."

THE IDEA THAT GOD CREATED HUMANKIND IN HIS IMAGE IS AN accepted spiritual principle in all major religions. This powerful belief in the inherent divine worth of humanity has been at the heart of all humanistic religious thinkers. But for Rav Kook, a person's love of God must affect not only one's relationship to human beings, but also one's relationship to all of God's creatures, including animals.

Rav Kook did not endorse the condescending attitude that animals exist to become food and clothing for human beings. While it is true that a human's life takes priority over an animal's, Rav Kook asks us to imagine a world where we can thrive without the need to kill animals.

In this chapter, Rav Kook will explain to us how being concerned for animals is not simply a liberal, Western value, but rather, it is a manifestation of a person's spiritual sensitivity to God's creatures. All of the pieces in this chapter excluding the first and the last four pieces come from one essay Rav Kook wrote called "Chazon Hatzimchonut v'Hashalom." This essay was compiled by Rav David Cohen (the Nazir).

Animal Rights Are a Spiritual Value

A Great Love
The heart of a *tzaddik* (righteous person) is filled with a great love for all creatures: the righteous and the wicked, Jews and non-Jews, and even toward all animals... (SK 3:170)

God Has Compassion on All His Creatures
There is a highly moral part of human evolution that exists in our generation due to the present culture. To be sure, it exists only as a utopian dream in the most extreme idealists. Nevertheless, it is a natural moral desire of righteous sensitivity: to be concerned for the justice of animals in all its implications.

We are told that the holy Rabbi Yehuda Hanasi was punished with a sickness because he told a calf being led to slaughter that had tried to hide beneath his garment, "Go! For this is what you were created for." He was only healed after an incident in which he demonstrated compassion for a group of weasels (*Bava Metzia* 85a).

Surely it is impossible to imagine that the Master of all beings, Who "has compassion on His creatures" (Tehillim 145:9), would create an eternal law within His creation, which is called "very good" (Bereishit 1:31), that makes it impossible for humankind to survive without distorting its moral sensitivity by murdering animals.

Man's Original Diet Was Vegetarian
There is no doubt for any sophisticated and logical thinker that the statement "And you will control the fish of the sea, the birds of the sky, the animals on earth, and all living insects that crawl on the ground" (Bereishit 1:26) does not imply a type of cruel tyranny that oppresses creatures in order to obtain selfish desires. *Chalilah* (God forbid) that a cruel, eternal law of slavery should be sealed in God's world, "Who is good to all, and compassionate on all of His creations" (Tehillim 145:9), and Who declared, "The world shall be built upon kindness" (Tehillim 89:3).

Rav Kook ate meat only on Shabbat.

In fact, the Torah has already testified that in the past, humankind did possess this highly moral trait. As Chazal explain (*Sanhedrin* 59b), Adam Harishon was not permitted to eat meat: "I have given you every tree…yielding seed for food" (Bereishit 1:29). Only after the children of Noach survived the flood was meat permitted to them: "Every living, moving thing will be yours to eat; like the vegetation, I have given you everything" (Bereishit 9:3).

Can we possibly imagine that we have forever lost that highly moral sensitivity that was once our inheritance? In response to such matters it is written, "I will bring wisdom from afar, and I will ascribe righteousness to my Creator" (Iyov 36:3).

Eating Meat Is a Compromise

While the Torah speaks of eating meat, it explains, "And when you crave meat and say, 'I desire some meat,' then you may eat as much of it as you want'" (Devarim 12:20). In this *pasuk* there is a subtle hint of criticism and call for restraint. In other words, *you may eat meat* as long as your inner sensitivity is not disgusted by eating the flesh of animals, as you are already disgusted by eating the flesh of people. For the latter, the Torah does not need to write an explicit prohibition. One does not need to be warned about that which is already ingrained in one as a natural truth. However, when the time does arrive when the inner moral sense of humankind precludes the eating of animals, then there will be no desire to eat meat, and thus we will not eat it. As it is written, "In a general statement of 'no' a 'yes' can be found, and in a general statement of 'yes,' a 'no'" (Sifri, Devarim 11).

The Torah Trains Us in Animal Sensitivity

The Subconscious Effect of Mitzvot

In order to prepare humankind for the ethical goals of the end of days, mitzvot involved with eating meat were instructed in a specific way. As the prophet Yeshayahu says, "All of your children will be taught by God, and great will be their peace. In righteousness, you will be established; be far from cruelty and you will have nothing to fear" (54:13–14). "You will have nothing to fear" because of the great distance from cruelty. This is not only talking about cruelty toward man, but cruelty toward all living creatures.

Covering the Blood (*Kisui Hadam*)

"If anyone of the Children of Israel or a convert who joins them traps an animal or bird that may be eaten and spills its blood, he must cover the blood with earth" (Vayikra 17:13).

The commandment to cover the blood of an animal or bird is a godly protest against the compromise that is given to the damaged soul; "for the inclination of man is bad from his youth" (Bereishit 8:21). It is with regard to the damaged soul that the Torah says, "And when you crave meat and say, 'I desire some meat,' then you may eat as much of it as you want" (Devarim 12:20). Concerning this person who shows no sign of any moral or righteous opposition to eating animals, the Torah says, *You are commanded to cover the blood* (Devarim 12:16). *Hide your embarrassment and weak morality.*

Even while one has not yet arrived at the appropriate moral level that would change one's practical lifestyle, even before reaching the height of piety (Chasidut) at which one would understand and deeply feel that it is not correct to take the life of an animal just to fulfill one's lusts, the mitzvot are preparing and training a person's moral sensitivity. Ultimately, humanity will actualize this ethical potential in its correct time.

Shechitah: Ethical Slaughter

Therefore, the very act of slaughtering (*shechitah*) needs to be sanctified with a special prayer. It must be done as carefully as possible in a way that minimizes pain to the animal in order to help a person internalize that one is not dealing with an object, some moving machine. Rather, this is a living and feeling creature, and a person needs to be sensitive to its feelings and emotions. One even needs to be aware of the feelings of this animal's family and the compassion it has on its offspring. This is the reason behind the prohibitions of killing an animal and its offspring on the same day and killing an animal that is very young, as well as the commandment of chasing away a mother bird before taking its eggs.

The godly wisdom behind the mitzvot is that they will bring with them a greater enlightenment in its appropriate time.

Animal Sacrifices (*Korbanot*)

In a "quiet, subtle voice" (1 Melachim 19:12), the kabbalists said, "In the future, animals will be on the level that human beings are on now through an elevation of worlds" (*Shaar Hamitzvot l'Arizal*).

Yet, as long as the ethical level of humankind has not been perfected... in that humankind does not even lift its head to be sensitive to animal rights... and as long as humankind still seeks to eat meat and to slaughter animals for its own satisfaction... even though this

Rav David Cohen (1887–1972), also known as "the Nazir of Jerusalem" (Photo courtesy Machon Nezer David). The Nazir was one of Rav Kook's closest students. Besides taking a religious vow to be a Nazirite, he was also a strict vegetarian. He is responsible for editing and publishing many of Rav Kook's philosophical and kabbalistic books, as well as this essay on vegetarianism.

is negative and undignified... then, for the time being, sacrifices can be used for an elevated function. Sacrifices help cultivate a feeling of gratitude to the Source of good: God.

But in the future, humankind's ethical sensitivity will ascend to such a level that positive laws will be given for the treatment of animals. In relation to this ideal level of ethical culture, the rabbis said a great and wondrous thing: "In the future, all of the sacrifices will be nullified" (*Midrash Tanchuma*, Emor 19). In addition, the Torah, when speaking about the end of days, says, "And the offering [*minchah*] of Yehuda and Yerushalayim will be sweet to God" (Malachi 3:4). The *pasuk* goes out of its way to emphasize the word *minchah*, which refers to a bread offering, instead of *korban*, which refers to an animal offering.

The Ideal Vegetarian Diet and Its Dangers

What Does the Ideal World Look Like?

At the end of days, there will be an inner thirst within humankind to do acts of righteousness. One will desire to pour out a spirit of kindness onto others, but none who need it will be found. Humanity will already be living a life of true happiness and success physically, ethically, and intellectually. At that time, humankind will turn to its lower brothers, the mute and downtrodden animals. Mankind will use its treasure of wisdom and experience to help teach and improve animals according to their abilities in physical, intellectual, ethical, and spiritual realms.

In our current era, which is filled with degradation and darkness, we cannot even imagine what this level of existence will look like. Animals will take on a new form, and the world will have a new shape. "If *tzaddikim* desire, they can create a world" (*Sanhedrin* 65b). This is the wondrous image that the prophets envisioned in relation to the culture of animals: "The wolf will live with the lamb; the leopard will lie down with the goat; the calf, lion, and the young together. A little child will lead them. The cow will feed with the bear; their young will lie down together, and the lion will eat straw like the ox. The infant will play near the snake's den, and the young child will put its hand into the snake's nest. They will neither harm nor destroy on all my holy mountain, for the earth will be filled with the knowledge of God as the waters cover the sea" (Yeshayahu 11:6–9).

Dangers of Self-Righteous Vegetarianism

However, let it be known that if a full moral obligation were to exist between people and animals at a time when humankind was still severely deficient in moral perfection, it would cause much negativity. In fact, it would be a stumbling block for our moral development. Humanity has a natural moral yearning that demands to be expressed; it even knocks on the heart of evil people. These people also feel forced to quench their natural thirst for righteousness. This is why we sometimes find a cruel leader will focus on a specific ethical ideal, and even find joy in fulfilling certain virtuous acts. For in doing so, he appeases the morality that pulsates within him.

If pious treatment of animals becomes a public norm and desire within society before the correct time, it will bring with it many necessary evils. For example, we may encounter many cruel people who would hurt and slaughter human beings without mercy. When their moral conscience comes to overwhelm them with guilt, they will pacify it with their righteous behavior toward animals. Man's sophisticated ability to commit evil would find in this an opening to justify many terrible deeds.... This would only strengthen the hands of cruel people. There is no end to the amount of confusion, negativity, pain, and injustice that would come about due to this prematurely becoming a social norm.

Therefore, godly wisdom decided that in order to create a firm path to morality, it was necessary to temporarily disconnect humans from animals. This is in order to keep our focus on humanitarian morality, because only through this will it be possible to bring true happiness at the end of days when humankind will arrive at an awareness of its relationship toward all its animal companions in creation. At that time, humankind will realize what pure morality looks like, and that it no longer requires any concessions. As it is written, "On that day I will make a covenant for them with the beasts of the field, the birds in the sky, and the creatures that move along the ground. I will abolish bow, sword, and battle from the land" (Hoshea 2:20).

Ethical Guidance during *Shechitah*

A letter to Rabbi Dr. Binyamin Menashe Levin (a student of Rav Kook, a Talmud scholar and author of *Otzar Hageonim*), December 31, 1908

It goes against the pure emotions of a *talmid chacham* and a spiritual person to be constantly involved in slaughtering animals. Even though currently, killing and eating animals is still necessary for the world, it is more fitting for the killing to be done by people who have not yet developed their emotional sensitivity. However, the ethical and wise ones should be overseers to make sure that the killing is not done in a barbaric way. The process of eating animals will then be accomplished in an elevated manner, so that in its proper time, it will enlighten the world. (IR 1, p. 230)

Rav Kook's Own Diet

These last three pieces are quoted from Moshe Nachmani's *Chai Ro'i* (Jerusalem: *Or Ha'orot*, 2015), a book dedicated to the topic of Rav Kook's understanding of vegetarianism.

Not to Obligate the Community

Rabbi Kivelevitz was a young student in Rav Kook's yeshiva in the city of Yaffo. When Rabbi Kivelevitz decided to become a vegetarian, he went to his rabbi, Rav Kook, to discuss it with him. Rav Kook praised him for his abstinence and said the following: "The Torah says, 'And when you have a lust for meat' (Devarim 12:20). That is to say, eating meat is only a matter of lust." Rav Kook added, "Unfortunately, I myself cannot be a vegetarian, in order not to obligate the rest of the community to hold back from eating meat."

Vegetarian during the Week

Rabbi Shaar Yashuv Cohen said that Rav Kook held back from eating meat during the week for ethical reasons (as is written in his essay, "Chazon Hatzimchonut v'Hashalom"), and only on Shabbat would he eat meat or chicken.

Idealism versus Realism

Rav Kook's son, Rav Tzvi Yehuda, explained that his father preferred not to eat meat at all – even during Shabbat – however, since he was a halachic authority and communal leader, Rav Kook believed it was not right that he should forbid himself that which is permissible for others.

Uniting the Four Songs

17

Rav Kook's Own Inner World

"Do not create 'Kookniks' for me."

WE CAN LEARN SO MUCH FROM STUDYING THE INSPIRATIONAL life of Rav Kook – his love of God, the Jewish people, and the entire world. And yet, there is a danger in focusing on individual people. We tend to idolize our role models. We blow them up into visions of perfection to whom no one can compare. When we place a hero on a level that is incomparable to anything in our lives, we take away that person's humanness and ability to be relevant to our own growth. I am sure that this comes from a good place, but the consequences are immense.

If Rav Kook has never experienced sadness, then how can he teach us how to confront sadness? If Rav Kook has never had doubts about God, then how can he teach us how to confront our doubts about God? When we make our role models perfect, we undermine our own ability to learn from them.

How do we find the balance of having role models but not idolizing them? In this chapter, Rav Kook reveals what incredible spiritual heights he reached, but also his own personal struggles. He thus makes himself eternally relevant to us as a model for our own spiritual growth.

The Angelic Rav Kook

I Must Speak about Everything
I feel forced to speak about everything, even about the highest heights; even if it is higher than my worth, my understanding, and my feelings. I am being pulled by an impulse within my soul. (SK 6:106)

My Words Come from a Higher Place
I sense that my words and letters come from a higher place, from the Source of life. (C, p. 58)

My Unique Spiritual Mission
It is not by chance that the God of all souls planted within me a continuous desire for everything hidden, moral, and spiritual. And it is not by chance that He brought me to the land of Israel; and it is not by chance that He created within me a spirit of courage and inner purity. Now, even though I am filled with endless weaknesses and imperfection – more than all the masses and all the regular religious people, and perhaps even more than all the most spiritual people who are sensitive to the movements of the soul – all of this [God] planted within me in order to illuminate the world. All of this is so I can create popular writings, which resonate with each individual, which are full of the light of the secrets of Torah. These [writings] will be full of poetry and strength, armed with a good mind and intellectual honesty. Such [writings] will bring a light to the nation of God, to save the world, which has begun to happen in the land of Israel. (SK 3:259)

I Am Not Afraid of Anyone
If I must be a person who argues with the entire world, because my soul is so drawn to truth that it cannot bear any type of lie, then it is impossible for me to be anyone else. I need to actualize the prin-

ciples of truth that are hidden deep within my spirit, without any consideration of whether the world agrees with me. This is the way of a seeker of truth who is inspired by a higher strength. (C, p. 158)

My Soul Is Connected to My People
Listen to me, my people. I am speaking to you from my soul, from the soul of my soul. I am connected to you by my very connection to life, and you are all connected to me. This is something that I feel more strongly than any other emotion: that you, only you, only all of you, all of your souls, all of the generations, are the essence of my life.... Without you I am nothing. (SK 1:163)

I Love Everyone
I love all people. I will never change this quality of mine. In every single person, I can find a good quality – literally in every one. (C, p. 191)

Arms the Size of the World
An open letter to the moshavim of the Galilee, September 23, 1913

My beloved brothers, if only I had arms the size of the world, so that I could hug you all with love. (IR 2, p. 229)

To Hug All of Humanity
From a conversation Rav Kook had with the Israeli writer Azar, the head of the Organization of Jewish Writers in the Land of Israel

If only the whole of humanity could be placed into one single body so that I could hug everyone. (Quoted in Rav Shlomo Aviner, *B'Ahavah v'Emunah*, p. 105)

Being Compassionate toward Nature
This is a story told by Rabbi Aryeh Levin about an incredible interaction he had with Rav Kook.

I recall the early days from 1905 onward, when it was granted me by the Grace of God, the Blessed One, to go up to the Holy Land, and I came to Jaffa. There I first went to visit our great master Rabbi Avraham Isaac Kook, who received me with good cheer, as it was his hallowed [holy] custom to receive everyone. We chatted together on themes of Torah study. After an early Minchah (afternoon prayer service), he went out, as his hallowed custom was, to stroll a bit in the fields and gather his thoughts; and I went along. On the way, I plucked some branch or flower. Our great master was taken aback; and he told me gently, "Believe me: In all my days I have taken care never to pluck a blade of grass or flower needlessly, when it had the ability to grow or blossom. You know the teaching of our Sages that there is not a single blade of grass below, here on earth, which does not have a heavenly force [or angel] above telling it, 'Grow!' Every sprout and leaf of grass says something, conveys some meaning. Every stone whispers some hidden message in the silence. Every Creation utters its song [in praise of the Creator]." Those words, spoken from a pure and holy heart, engraved themselves deeply upon my heart. From that time on I began to feel a strong sense of compassion for everything. (Simcha Raz, *A Tzaddik in Our Time* [Jerusalem: Feldheim, 1976], pp. 108–9)

This Is How You Should Learn Torah
A letter to Rabbi Shmuel Hakohen Kook (Rav Kook's brother), 1898

Your letter has caused my heart great happiness after waiting so long for its arrival. I am so pleased that you have informed me about your learning. Nevertheless, I was totally shocked when I saw that you only review your learning three times.

Know this, my precious brother: after much experience I am certain that it is impossible to benefit from one's learning by reviewing it only three times. I strongly request that you, my precious brother, train yourself to review each chapter at least ten times before beginning a new one. Indeed, there is absolutely no benefit to having learned something that will be forgotten immediately after. I won't say any more. (IR 1, p. 9)

Prophecy in Israel Continues into Exile

In 1914 Rav Kook was invited to speak at Agudat Yisrael's Knessiah Hagedolah (Great Assembly) in Frankfurt, Germany. After debating with his family and students whether or not he should leave Israel for an entire month, he eventually decided that he must go, since it was an incredible opportunity to help strengthen Diaspora Jewry's love of the land of Israel. Shortly after Rav Kook arrived in Germany, World War I broke out, and all paths of transportation back to Palestine were cut off. Struggling to deal with being forced out of the land of Israel, Rav Kook wrote this piece describing his inner experience.

The experience of *ruach hakodesh* (divine inspiration) that happens in the land of Israel is a permanent event, even if a person is forced out of Israel due to a mistake or an urgent necessity, just as prophecy that was encountered in the land of Israel does not discontinue even outside of Israel: "The word of God came to Yechezkel (*Hayo haya davar Hashem el Yechezkel*) in the land of Kasdim" (Yechezkel 1:3). The rabbis explain that the double language of *"hayo haya"* teaches that the word of God had already come to him before.

    The extent to which one cannot bear the atmosphere outside of Israel, the extent to which a person feels the spirit of impurity in an impure land, is the extent to which he has absorbed the holiness of the land of Israel. (O, "Eretz Yisrael" 6)

God Will Not Abandon Me in Exile

Even though I am stuck in exile – even though I suffer great pains, both physical and spiritual – the kindness of God will not abandon me. I need to elevate myself to a higher freedom, to that which I had with me in the land of Israel. (C, p. 185)

My Heart Yearns for the Land of Israel
The heart yearns for the consciousness of the land of Israel, for the faith of the land of Israel, for the holiness of the land of Israel. Where can I get the joy of the land of Israel, the inner peace of the land of Israel, the divine connection of the land of Israel, the truth of the land of Israel, the courage of the land of Israel, the inner trust of the land of Israel? Give shade to me, God. God of mercy, please have compassion on me. Give me the merit to fully return to You; please return me to Your beautiful land. (SK 6:71)

Even in Exile
Thank God, the atmosphere of the land of Israel has come to me even in exile. (C, p. 185)

A Revival of Prophecy
The sprouts of prophecy are growing, *bnei nevi'im* (the descendants of prophets) are awakening, and the spirit of prophecy is rising in Israel. It is searching for a sanctuary. It desires mighty spirits, full of strength and holiness, who know how to feed the word, announce the truth of truths, and who will tell how the word of God was revealed to them, neither lying nor flattering, revealing their spirit with faith. It will be known that it is not lies that motivate the pen, and it is not deceit that wears the guise of self-confidence. (OK 1, p. 157)

The Controversial Censored Paragraph
For many years, this spiritually provocative piece was censored, and very few people knew it existed. Eventually it was published in *Shemoneh Kevatzim* in 1999. It has since been the discussion point of many essays. Does this piece hint that Rav Kook thought he had received prophecy? It is difficult to say a strong yes or no; nevertheless, this piece does show that Rav Kook was struggling with the question.

I listen and I hear from the depths of my soul, from among the feelings of my heart, the voice of God calling. I experience a great trembling; have I so descended as to become a *navi sheker* (false prophet), to say God sent me when the word of God has not been revealed to me? Yet I feel my soul yearning as the growth of prophecy increases. (SK 4:17)

The Humanized Rav Kook

My Inner War
Whoever said that my soul is torn spoke well. Certainly, it is torn. It is impossible for us to imagine a human being whose soul is not torn. Only an inanimate object is whole. A human being is full of opposing desires, an inner war that rages inside constantly. A person's entire struggle is to unify the torn parts of his or her soul through a greater vision that includes everything. Only then will one move toward harmony. (C, p. 228)

I Ignore Myself
I force myself to learn, act, socialize, to carry out various obligations until not a single thought ever gets the opportunity to become complete and mature. The time has come to break the chains that I myself have placed on the limbs of my soul. I must stop paying attention to external obstacles; salvation is always in my heart. The wellspring of happiness is constantly flowing; God's kindness fills the world. I must stand up for my inner understanding and pay attention to the secret language of creativity that dwells in my inner chambers. I will listen and my soul will be revived. (C, p. 18)

I Must Understand Myself
I need to speak a lot about myself; matters of my essence must become very clear to me. Through understanding myself I will

understand everything – the world, life – until I reach the source of life. (SK 7:189)

I Don't Have Time to Write for Myself
A letter to Rav Kook's friend Rabbi Yitzchak Levi (secretary of Merkaz HaRav Yeshiva and one of its cofounders), September 26, 1913

Concerning your request that I put aside time to reply to your letter in depth: please believe me that due to my many obligations... I do not have the strength to do this. The fact is that due to a lack of time, even the things that I truly desire to write down for myself, I have no time for. (IR 2, p. 225)

The Struggles of Being a Rabbi
A letter to Rabbi Dr. Yosef Zeliger (head of the Achva Cheder, the forerunner of the Tachkemoni School in Yaffo), November 15, 1906

Writing, and specifically writing letters, is very hard work for me. It is connected to many things that are bothering me – the fact that I am enslaved to the important work that is on my shoulders, the service of being a rabbi of the rabbinical court of the new Yishuv in our ancestors' land. This job is filled with many different types of work: great hopes and thoughts that inspire the heart and expand the soul... but also things that depress the heart and exhaust the soul....

These things are sometimes a great obstacle to the spiritual development of the spirit. This heavy work of the rabbinate is also affecting my writing. And so, I am unable to fulfill my most precious obligations of writing letters. I have no control over this. And any person with a good heart should judge me favorably. (IR 1, p. 38)

I Have No One to Talk To
A letter to Rabbi Shmuel Hakohen Kook (Rav Kook's brother), December 27, 1907

Many days have passed and I have not written to you, my friend, due to the many burdens of my soul. You know how great my desire is when it comes to matters of spirituality. Yet due to my many mistakes, I have not actualized anything.

I don't have anyone here to speak to and pour out my heart to; no one is able to come close to the inner point of my desires – neither older people nor younger people. And this exhausts me. (IR 1:128)

I Have an Inclination toward Sadness
My broken and damaged heart – my inclination toward sadness – comes about because I cannot find satisfaction in anything in the world unless it has a spark of divine light, an encounter with the pleasantness of divine holiness. And when God's light is hidden and concealed, I experience intense suffering; it is very bitter for me. "From the depths, I call out to God" (Tehillim 130:1). (SK 6:72)

All Limitations Frustrate Me
My soul cannot place itself in any form of limit – even the limits of Torah and the fear of God – unless they become refined and rise to the purest yearnings of the soul. (SK 8:208)

I Want to Liberate My Soul
I want to break out from all the limits of intellectual blocks. I want to liberate my individual soul as well as the collective soul from any unnecessary fear, distorted arrogance, false humility, and self-deception. I am searching for pathways to a great freedom; but will I find them? Who knows? I have lifted up my eyes; only God has the salvation to help those without strength, like me. (C, p. 45)

I Am Not a Practical Person
A letter to Rabbi Dov Ber Hakohen Kook (Rav Kook's brother, the first rabbi of Afula and the head of Machon Harry Fischel, the Harry Fischel Institute for Research in Jewish Law), July 8, 1909

I will not refrain from telling you, my precious brother, that in the last few days, I have begun, with the help of God, to actualize some of my ideas concerning the "Merkaz Yeshiva" in the New Yishuv.... However, the hardest part of this is the practical element. It involves financial issues, which are certainly not my expertise. Even the relatively spiritual element of creating a curriculum is also contrary to my nature. (IR 1, p. 261)

I Do Not Deal with Details

A letter to the Palestine Land Development Company (the association for acquiring land in Israel), October 6, 1911

I hope it is clear, concerning any practical matters that I refer to, that I do not desire to accept any responsibility. As you know, I am only able to deal with the spirit of our holy land and the revival of our holy people upon it. But I do not deal in details. I would be very happy if through my words of inspiration, practical matters would take care of themselves. (IR 2, p. 50)

Despite Rav Kook being a self-described introvert, his role as the chief rabbi of Israel forced him to be a very public person. He struggled with this tension his entire life. Here, Rav Kook is sitting with Nahum Sokolow (*right*), the secretary general of the World Zionist Organization (1928).

I Do Not Want to Be a Rabbi

A letter to Rav Yechiel Michel Tukachinsky (principal and head of Etz Chaim and author of *Gesher Hachaim*), July 25, 1907

I have an obligation to my soul to reveal to you its true desires. Since Rabbi Yitzchak Blazer passed away, it seems that there is a need to appoint a new head of the *kollel*.[1] Now, since matters of the rabbinate are contrary to my very personality and talents, and I honestly yearn to sit in the holy land of Israel without the burden of providing rabbinical rulings for the community, perhaps you can suggest my offer to whom it may concern. For if you are able to appoint lowly me to this position of head of the *kollel*, in my humble opinion, I believe I would be well suited to it. I think that in this job I would find my true dream of dwelling in the holy city of Jerusalem without the burden of the rabbinate and all of its responsibilities.

If you have an answer, I hope that you will not delay in responding to me. But if there are obstacles, let it be as if these words were never said. (IR 1, p. 89)

I Miss My Wife

In 1889, not long after Rav Kook became the rabbi of Zeimel, Lithuania, his wife Batsheva contracted a fatal disease and passed away at age twenty-two, leaving him with a one-and-a-half-year-old daughter named Freida Chanah. Rav Kook struggled to deal with the pain of losing his wife. This is part of a poem he wrote about her.[2]

---

1. A *kollel* is an institution for full-time Torah study that is financially supported by the community.
2. To help me translate this difficult poem, I relied on Yehudah Mirsky's translation for guidance. His original translation can be found in his brilliant doctoral dissertation: "An Intellectual and Spiritual Biography of Rabbi Avraham Yitzhaq Ha-Cohen Kook from 1865 to 1904" (Harvard University, March 2007), pp. 158–59.

Shadows surround me, and darkness descends; fog thickens, the sun becomes dim for me.

The sun shines, rays of light emanate; yet for me they are dark. O Heavens!

[She] lies in the grave, but is still alive; there is no end to the heartbreak, for agony never stops....

I cry out loud, deafen ears, breathe into the dust, and it rises to heaven.

Thoughts of confusion, great is the turmoil. That my soul was abandoned, in its crooked path.

To the light, it seems that I have been saved. I will immerse myself in Torah, because her face I can no longer imagine.

My longing hope, from your lovely friendship; here it is burned, like a pure sacrifice.

...Like a pillar of light floating in the air, it passed by so fast and has now disappeared. And just before she dried up, she gave birth to a daughter for me. (PR 1, pp. 80–83)

I Miss My Daughter

A letter to Rabbi Shlomo Zalman Pines (prominent rabbi in Zurich, Switzerland), March 20, 1920

After being stuck in Europe for five long years without his three daughters, on August 29, 1919, Rav Kook returned to Israel. Less than two months later, on October 21, 1919, his twelve-year-daughter, Esther Yael, fell down a flight of stairs at their home in Jerusalem, broke her neck, and died immediately. Rav Kook was brokenhearted; years of dreaming to reunite with his little girl, and now she was gone forever. Not long after her death, Rav Kook wrote this letter to a friend.

I really have to apologize to you concerning the delay of my letter. However, there is a reason for this. You must already have heard about the terrible and shocking tragedy that happened to us immediately as we returned to the holy land. Our precious and beautiful daughter was taken from us in the most terrifying and sudden way; it has left an extremely deep wound in our souls. May God have compassion.... (IR 4, p. 48)

I Worry about My Friends

A letter to Rabbi Yaakov Moshe Charlap (one of Rav Kook's closest students, who served as the *rosh yeshiva* of Mercaz HaRav), August 11, 1910

I want to request something from you, my honorable and good friend: that you will not cause yourself any emotional suffering or monetary damages by letting it be known publicly that we have a loyal friendship and a strong soul connection.

At a time when my enemies have greatly increased, due to our people's many sins, "your friendship is more important to me than wine" (Shir Hashirim 1:2). May the Rock of Israel reveal to us the light and joy of His redemption and holiness. May we all be comforted in Jerusalem.

The small and unimportant Avraham Yitzchak Hakohen Kook (IR 1, p. 360)

I Worry about My Parents

A letter to Rav Kook's parents, Rav Shlomo Zalman and Perel Zlata Kook, June 30, 1910

I only desire that my beloved parents be full of life and not, God forbid, suffer due to the controversy concerning my involvement with the *shemittah* settlements. Believe me, there is nothing to be pained over. Our holy land is being built in front of our very eyes. This is the word of God that was sent by His messengers the prophets concerning the return to Zion and the revival of the Jewish people in the holy land.

All we are trying to do, with the help of God, is to take a part, whether big or small, in this great event. This is such an enormous honor that even with all the negative criticism and unpleasant feelings, it is still worth it. I must thank God for giving me the type of soul that is able to dedicate itself to such holy events at such an important period of history.

God forbid that you, my beautiful parents, should become brokenhearted even in the smallest way due to the pain of these things. I only hope to God that all these matters, which for me are not an embarrassment but rather an honor and privilege, should awaken sleeping souls to serve God and His people in the holy land. (IR 1, p. 352)

I Struggle to Write Clearly
A letter to Rabbi Dr. Binyamin Menashe Levin (a student of Rav Kook, a Talmud scholar, and author of *Otzar Hageonim*), July 28, 1909

I have to confess that I am not capable of writing clearly. On the other hand, I am not jealous of those writers who are able to express everything in a simple and structured form. Matters of true depth can only be expressed clearly if they are condensed and simplified. This is the limitation of language in expressing our thoughts.

However, we will never be able to totally explain deep ideas. Indeed, do we truly desire to argue with the Divine Being Who designed reality such that profound ideas are "sustained in the world of secrets"? Both the *Zohar* (the famous book on kabbalah) and the *Guide for the Perplexed* (the Rambam's famous book on philosophy) agree that language functions merely as hints and road signs.

We often see that a person who tries to express everything proves just how shallow his inner spirit is. Our words should be patient. The soul must be trained to sense the subtle hints within words. Only then will the tool of speech be transformed into a power that gives life.

I want to pour out my soul in whatever form it takes. And I am not so worried about the editing demands, which you know are difficult for me. We must send out words full of life from among our people. They must be words that are spoken with confidence, full of the soul of the nation and the Divine Presence within it. We must have no fear and anxiety due to any external disapproval. (IR 1, p. 267)

I Struggle to Write with a Deadline
A letter to Rabbi Shmuel Hakohen Kook (Rav Kook's brother), February 4, 1908

Many things are blocking me from taking action and writing. There is a great burden, both physical and spiritual, that I feel upon me. May God give me peace of mind so that I can give every matter and idea its right time and place.

I need to think a lot and to act and write very little. Only then will I calm my spirit. Unfortunately, the circumstances force me to speak, act, and sometimes to write under external pressure. But I have no skill for this. I am no academic who has developed his abilities. God has given me a divine gift, but it must be allowed to spread out independently within me without any external demands.

When my words become materialized on a page with this relaxed spirit, I begin to see the divine fruits and blessings of my gift. However, if I lay down the heavy hand of editing and proofreading, I find my poor and deficient mind unable to create anything. (IR 1, p. 154)

I Want to Publish My Diaries Unedited
A letter to Rabbi Tzvi Yehuda Kook (Rav Kook's son, who served as the *rosh yeshiva* of Mercaz HaRav), May 25, 1914

Thank God, yesterday was the 28th of Iyar, the incredible day on which God gave us the merit of coming to His beautiful land...[3]

I have been overcome by an inner desire to publish some of my

---

3. Rav Kook originally arrived in Israel on this exact day in 1904, ten years before.

diary entries in their original form. I have decided to publish them by the name *Arpelei Tohar* (Illuminating Clouds). How many pages will it be? I don't know. I only hope that these words, just as they are, without any form of editing, will be a blessing. In fact, perhaps their blessing will be manifested specifically through the lack of editing. "Like warm bread taken on the day of baking" (1 Shmuel 21:7). (IR 2, pp. 292–93)

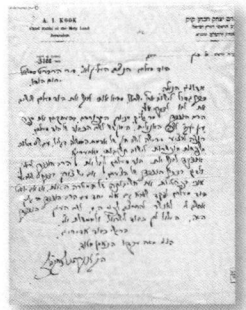 

As the chief rabbi of Israel, Rav Kook was constantly pressured to write letters and articles. Here (*left*) is an original letter in Rav Kook's own handwriting. Rav Kook would write his thoughts down in a diary during every free moment. His only son, Rav Tzvi Yehuda (*right*), spent most of his life editing and publishing his father's writings.

Rav Kook the Teacher

A True Master
A true master... must be so dedicated to improving the lives of each of his disciples that due to his great love and dedication... he has an inner understanding of the essence of each of those who dwell under his flag... (EA, *Berachot* 1 p. 133)

A Rabbi Is a Servant to His People
A servant to a holy people on a holy land.[4]

---

4. This was a common way Rav Kook would sign his letters.

A Description of a Righteous Leader

> Shmuel the Righteous would travel to all the homes of Israel and conduct court cases in their cities. As it is written, "He would travel each year and circle Beit El, the Galil, and Mitzpeh, in order to judge the cases of the Jewish people" (1 Shmuel 7:16). (*Shabbat* 56a)

The best national leaders are those who are so focused on helping their people that they are aware of the personal significance, lifestyle, and specific needs of each person. These leaders do not simply look at the people from their own subjective perspective, but instead, it is as if they reach down to the people's lives, almost as if they are standing with the people in their exact situation.

When this extremely important character trait increases in righteous leaders, it pulls them to their people, motivating them to travel and visit their people's homes. These leaders must humble their spirits in order to understand lifestyles that may not be familiar to them.... The righteous leaders must guide their people with justice and inner strength, and not through external law enforcement that focuses on superficial details, relying on a fear of rules....

This was the greatness that the prophet Shmuel was blessed with. His spirit caused him to travel to all the cities and houses of the Jewish people, in order to meet them in their situations, in order to elevate them. He did not attempt to influence them from a lofty distance. (EA, *Shabbat* 2, p. 52)

Teacher and Student Help Each Other

Yechidei segula (powerful souls), visionaries, and the most sophisticated and idealistic people need to draw close to the masses with a sense of humility. These individuals must recognize that not only must they help and influence the masses, but they also must learn from and be influenced by them.

The natural health – both physical and spiritual – that exists in the masses is greater than that found among these spiritual visionaries. The great thoughts and spiritual exertions of these special individuals have damaged their souls' simplicity, calmness, and purity. (SK 3:78)

I Believe in the Goodness of People
The fallen souls who come to me give me strength. I have compassion on them; I want the best for them.... They thirst for God's light and goodness. They are happy to have someone who will tell about their honesty, someone who will stand up for them.

I know that deep within these fallen souls, the light of God is burning, a higher spirit is breathing; in the depths of their souls they desire to walk in the path of light, the path of honesty and goodness. I am certain that eventually the help of God will come, and God's light and goodness will come to them. (SK 6:86)

The Danger of Worshiping Your Hero
Devekut b'tzaddikim (attaching oneself to righteous people), in order that the power within their righteous souls will mix with the incomplete soul, is an extremely valuable tool in spiritual development. However, one must be very careful. For if one makes a mistake with a righteous person, and becomes completely attached to him to the point of also attaching to his flaws, these flaws will sometimes express themselves far more negatively in the loyal follower than they did in the leader himself.

Fortunate is the Jew who is connected to the soul of the nation, which is only good, in order to draw through it the divine light. (O, "Yisrael" 3.3)

The World Does Not Understand Me
I am certain that the world does not understand my value, the depth of my intellect, and the breadth of my thoughts. In the same way, they do not understand my faults, my deficiencies, my imperfections, and the flaws of my mind. (C, p. 162)

Do Not Create "Kookniks"
Do not create "Kookniks" for me. Any Jew who is dedicated to helping the Torah and Judaism is one of us. (*Nefesh Hare'iyah l'Shloshah b'Elul* 1:46)

Do Not Restrict Me to One Group
If I wished, I could attract a group of followers to myself (who would be considered my Chasidim), who would spread my teachings and thoughts. But I do not want to restrict myself in such a way. I want to connect to the entire Jewish people, and in no way do I desire to be disconnected from any person. (MoR, p. 170)

Postscript

A Spiritual Letter to the Reader

DEAR READER,

If you have already read this far in the book, you will know that Rav Kook does not simply describe Judaism; rather, he challenges his readers to be active members of his spiritual revolution. Rav Kook is not interested in merely conveying information, nor purely giving inspiration; instead, he desires to use the power of his pen to cause a transformation in the individual, nation, and the entire world.

If you are one of the many spiritual seekers who have been touched by the power of Rav Kook's words and desire to be a part of his spiritual revolution, here is a list of seventeen revolutionary issues upon which we must focus.

One: The Individual

Religion will not survive if it remains a society of robots who blindly follow external instructions. Rav Kook rejects the idea that religion is about conformity and obedience. Instead, he challenges us to seek personal and individual meaning in our spirituality. If we are truly interested in changing the world around us, we must first be concerned with individual transformation. Indeed, the danger of being too selfless is that when we have no self, we also have no self to give to others.

> It is impossible for us to speak about a national revolution if we do not first speak about the revolution of each unique individual. (O, "Yisrael" 7.17)

We need a spiritual revolution in our understanding of and relationship to the individual.

Two: Torah

Unfortunately, there are those who teach the Torah in an impersonal way, as historical episodes or an exercise of the mind that has little to say in answer to the student's actual spiritual dilemmas. As a consequence, there is a growing number of religious people who are bored and uninspired, and may even eventually leave the life of Torah.

In Rav Kook's time, he witnessed a movement of religious Jews rejecting their tradition because of such an impersonal relationship to the Torah. As a reaction, Rav Kook called us to return to studying the Torah in a way that speaks directly to each person's unique soul and personality. The Torah must be practical and relevant, giving solutions for one's specific struggles.

> One must know that one will never be satisfied unless special attention is given to that which one's soul demands. Only then will one be successful in serving God with a truly deep sense of happiness. (OT 9:12)

We need a spiritual revolution in our understanding of and relationship to the Torah.

Three: God

When we are children, we relate to God as if He is an invisible man in the sky – as if He is a bigger and more powerful version of our parents. Yet the more we grow and develop, the less we can accept such an immature concept of God.

Rav Kook believed that atheism was in fact an unconscious search for a deeper and more sophisticated understanding of God. And therefore, Rav Kook advises religion not to fight with atheism, but to listen and learn. Atheism may not have the ultimate answer to the meaning of life, but it helps destroy false idols.

> **When a person understands the profound criticism of faith that atheism offers, one is able to transform its destructive force into a drive for return to the true God. (O, "Zeronim" 5)**

We need a spiritual revolution in our understanding of and relationship to God.

Four: The Meaning of Life

It is not enough to be inspired by an idea of spirituality here and there; what we seek is to comprehend the ultimate purpose of our lives – what am I doing here and why?

Rav Kook believed that we too often measure our life's success based on perfection, completion, and achieving an exact goal. He wrote that the purpose of life is not found in being perfect, but in constant growth. In other words, the meaning of our lives is not found in arriving at the end goal, but in the very journey of transformation.

Rav Kook argued that we do ourselves a disservice by imagining that happiness is only experienced by attaining perfection. Instead, he believed that ultimate joy is encountered through gradually evolving into a more perfect person each day.

> **A wise person understands that each and every step has the profound effect of bringing one to a greater level of perfection. This person knows that the very journey of reaching perfection should be valued and treasured. One who thinks this way will find a constant satisfaction and peace of mind in each and every step. (EA, *Berachot* 2, p. 33)**

We need a spiritual revolution in our understanding of and relationship to the meaning of life.

Five: *Teshuvah* and Personal Growth

Where do our sins and mistakes come from? Some religions teach that human beings are inherently evil; Freud argued that humanity is innately selfish. Either way, a common theme is that our flaws are something integral to our being; in this view anger, jealousy, and hate are essential parts of human nature. As a consequence of this theory, the way one should grow is by "overcoming" oneself, by "getting outside" of oneself, by doing battle with oneself.

But Rav Kook did not believe in this depressing and pessimistic understanding of human nature. Instead, he believed that all sins and mistakes come from one's alienation from one's true self. In other words, we become angry or jealous or hateful to relieve the pain of not being aligned with all we have truly become within.

And therefore, according to Rav Kook, the goal of all personal growth and *teshuvah* is not overcoming oneself, but returning to one's truest self – not getting outside of oneself, but being true to what is inside.

> The purpose of all personal growth is to put each and every power, potential, and talent in its correct place and not to confuse their natural order, thereby preventing their expression. God made both people and the world inherently good, providing them with all of the tools necessary to improve the body and the soul. Anyone who perverts the divine order can only cause damage and destruction. (MA 2.3)

We need a spiritual revolution in our understanding of and relationship to *teshuvah* and personal growth.

Six: Character Traits

Many personal growth books warn people against negative character traits such as anger, arrogance, jealousy, and depression, and encourage a person toward the attainment of good character traits such as humility, joy, and a readiness to forgive.

Now, although Rav Kook believed that the desire to grow is healthy, he stated that an unsophisticated path of growth was dangerous. A person can strive for humility and end up with low self-esteem; a person can strive to be forgiving and end up being self-effacing – and so on.

And therefore, Rav Kook argued that in order to experience true growth a person must first have a clear understanding of what the ideal goal would look like. Rav Kook therefore challenges us to define humility, happiness, and freedom, and only then to strive toward attaining them. Before one tries to remove anger, arrogance, jealousy, and depression, one must first understand what they are and where they come from.

This is one of Rav Kook's main insights: first define where you are going before beginning the journey of growth.

> **If one does not clearly comprehend a character trait, one will come to a superficial and extreme version of it. Therefore, it is of utmost importance that one investigates each character trait until one can distinguish between its real definition and that which is actually unrelated to it. (MA 3.1)**

We need a spiritual revolution in our understanding of and relationship to our *middot* (character traits).

Seven: Listening to the Inner Child

Are adults the only source of wisdom? Is old age a requirement for intelligence?

Rav Kook believed that although children must learn about consistency and responsibility from adults, there is much that adults need to learn from children. It is easy to grow up and give up, to become cynical and pessimistic about the world. Rav Kook believed that children are the great teachers of idealism. They refuse to give up; they are sincerely excited about all parts of life. Children remind adults not to take themselves too seriously, and that a meaningful life must be filled not only with important goals, but also wonder and joy.

And therefore, if we are truly interested in transforming the world into a better place, we must learn to listen to and protect not only our children, but also our inner child.

> **Any natural yearning a person has toward an idealistic dream is really a return to one's inner child. Within this yearning exists an attachment to an ideal that is devoid of any abstract justification. There is an impulse that comes from a place that is totally unconscious. And it is precisely this inner child that we must guard from all negative influences. (SK 351)**

We need a spiritual revolution in our understanding of and relationship to our inner child.

Eight: Prayer

If God knows everything, then why do we need to pray? If God loves us, then why would we need to convince Him to give us what we desire?

Rav Kook believed that all of these questions come from a basic misunderstanding of the role of prayer. In his eyes, the goal of prayer is not to change God's mind – which is impossible – but to change one's own mind. In other words, the main purpose of prayer is to use the spiritual power of speech to transform oneself into a person who is able to receive God's blessings.

According to Rav Kook, it is through the act of prayer that a person becomes able to receive the divine blessings of wisdom, health, and peace. Just as a sick person may be unable to stomach the most delicious food, so too, a person who is depressed and angry is unable to receive happiness into his or her life. Prayer is about transforming oneself into a person who is worthy of blessings; it is the power of prayer that turns us into a spiritual vessel that is able to receive all the good we are requesting.

> Each person praying should understand that the act of prayer is a miraculous law of nature that God created in His world for the purpose of bringing His creatures to every type of perfection.... It must be made clear: prayer is not something that influences God, Heaven forbid. (OR, "Tefillah" 2:2)

We need a spiritual revolution in our understanding of and relationship to prayer.

Nine: The Spiritual Importance of Creativity

Rav Kook believed that it is not enough for an idea to be true in order for it to be able to transform the world; there are many correct ideas that can be found in books that have never reached the ears of the masses. In Rav Kook's eyes, in order for an idea to change the world, it must also be communicated in a creative and imaginative form. In other words, it must be both true and beautiful, intelligent and attractive.

And thus, Rav Kook believed that in order to spread matters of the soul and effect change in the world, we must learn to appreciate the spiritual importance of creativity. The Torah must be taught not only in a true way, but also in a beautiful and attractive way. Following this logic, Rav Kook was convinced that the Mashiach would be a person of spectacular artistic genius. Listen to his incredible words:

> The beautiful and profound emotions of *teshuvah* (spiritual transformation) must be revealed though creative writing. This is in order that our revolutionary generation will understand *teshuvah* in the depths of their souls in a new and fresh way.... A singer of *teshuvah* will rise up. This person will be a singer of life, a singer of revolution. (OT 17:5)

We need a spiritual revolution in our understanding of and relationship to creativity.

Ten: Ethics and Concern for Others

In a time when radical and extreme religion threatens to destroy the entire world, Rav Kook provides a much-needed answer, combining a deep love of God with an uncompromising compassion for all human beings. In his eyes, increased spirituality must naturally lead to an expansion in ethics; God's presence in the world must become so real that to injure another human being would mean desecrating the divine image.

A person who reads the writings of Rav Kook will discover a man who rejected superficial labels of religious versus secular, right-wing versus left-wing. In Rav Kook's own life, he combined a deep love of God with an uncompromising compassion for all human beings.

> It is forbidden for the fear of heaven to push away the natural ethics of a person. And if it does do this, then it is not a pure fear of heaven. In fact, the sign of a pure fear of heaven is when natural ethics – which is planted within the honest nature of a person – grows and develops to even higher levels than it would have without it. (OK 3, introduction, p. 27)

We need a spiritual revolution in our understanding of and relationship to ethics.

Eleven: Zionism

In today's age, when people hear the word *Zionism*, they automatically think of politics. Now, obviously, political issues are of great importance; yet the exclusive focus on them is a distortion of what Zionism should be about.

In Rav Kook's eyes, the land of Israel is not only a piece of land that we own, but a spiritual atmosphere that we enter; it transforms who we are. We have focused so much on political Zionism that we have forgotten the importance of spiritual Zionism. While Herzl believed that the main reason a Jew should make aliyah to Israel is that it saves the person from the threat of anti-Semitism, Rav Kook believed that understanding Zionism simply as an *ir miklat* (place of refuge) is a distortion of Judaism.

Instead, Rav Kook asks us to return to Israel not only because of political motivations, but also due to the land's spiritual power, because there is something magical about living in Israel. It enables one to uncover one's soul, to meet one's essence, one's true self.

> The land of Israel is not just some external object, some material possession of the nation.... Rather, the essence of the land of Israel is tied to the very life of the Jewish people. (O, "Eretz Yisrael" 1)

We need a spiritual revolution in our understanding of and relationship to Zionism.

Twelve: The Holiness of the Body

On the surface, it seems as though the chapter name "The Holiness of the Body" is a careless editing mistake. Should not a book about religion include a chapter called "The Holiness of the Soul"? Usually people assume that religion focuses on the importance of the soul rather than on the importance of the body. The materialistic lusts of the body seem to distract a person from matters of the soul, and therefore the body is often seen as the enemy of spirituality. In fact, throughout the history of religion, many very pious individuals deprived and tortured their bodies in order to purify their souls.

Yet Rav Kook's understanding of the Torah caused him to disagree with this interpretation. Rav Kook asks his students to focus not only on the holiness of the soul, but also on the holiness of the body. The power of the soul is dependent on the strength of the body. When the body is weak, the soul cannot fully express itself. Therefore, according to Rav Kook, the body is not the enemy of the soul, but its closest companion.

To be sure, Rav Kook of course agreed that a person should not become so focused on the body that the soul becomes forgotten. The ideal goal of a spiritual seeker should be that the body and soul work together in a holistic way of serving God.

In this way, Rav Kook was very much ahead of his time; today, New Age spirituality often recommends using physical exercise, stretching, and healthy eating to reconnect a person to one's soul. Holistic spirituality has become a universal trend. It is truly incredible to think that as early as the beginning of the 1900s, Rav Kook was trying to help people realize that religion must also focus on the health of the body.[1]

The demand for physicality is enormous. We need healthy bodies. But we have been so focused on our souls that we have forgotten the holiness of the body. We have neglected our health

---

[1] To be sure, Rav Kook was not the originator of the Jewish belief in the spiritual importance of the body. There exist many statements from the Torah, Chazal, Rambam, *Kuzari*, and Chasidut on this topic. Much of the uniqueness of Rav Kook's spiritual revolution is not in its total originality, but in its courage to revive and apply ancient Jewish ideas that have been forgotten or ignored. In Rav Kook's own words, "The old will become new, and the new will become holy" (IR 1, p. 214). In fact, Rav Kook once said of himself, "There is nothing in my thoughts and opinions that does not have its source in the writings of the Ari [Rabbi Yitzchak Luria, a famous kabbalist]" (*Nefesh Hare'iyah l'Shloshah b'Elul* 1:46).

and strength, and have forgotten that we possess holy bodies no less than we possess holy souls. We have abandoned the life of practicality, the training of our senses, and our connection with the concrete material world. (O, "Hatechiyah" 33)

We need a spiritual revolution in our understanding of and relationship to the body.

Thirteen: Faith and Science

There is a never-ending discussion about faith and science being in contradiction – that the creation story, the Torah's account of the world being created in six days, is in opposition to modern science's theory of evolution. On the one hand, we hear atheists mock the sacred books of religion as archaic, scientifically and historically inaccurate. On the other hand, we hear religious fundamentalists deny basic scientific and historical evidence as a way of defending their sacred books. And therefore, the seeker of truth and spirituality may ask: Who is correct? Faith or science? God or humans?

Yet according to Rav Kook, this entire tension comes from a misunderstanding of the purpose of religion in general, and the Torah specifically. In his eyes, the goal of religion is not simply to tell historical and scientific facts, but rather, to communicate spiritual and ethical truths. In other words, the Torah was not written with the intention of merely imparting information, but rather, for the purpose of inspiring human transformation. And therefore, according to Rav Kook, to read the stories of the Torah in simply a literal fashion distorts the very essence of the Torah.

This would be like attempting to understand the phrase "You broke my heart" in a literal way. Obviously, when a person says to a lover, "You broke my heart," this is not a statement of medical fact describing a heart attack, but rather communicates intense emotional suffering.

In the same way, Rav Kook asks us to stop reading the Torah in an overly literal way, and instead begin uncovering its spiritual wisdom:

> Any person who has an honest mind must understand that even though these new truths are not absolutely proven, nevertheless, we certainly do not have any obligation to deny and reject them. Indeed, it is definitely not one of the goals of the Torah to simply tell facts and historical episodes. Instead, the main thing is the philosophical principles, the inner spiritual meaning. And thus, whenever there is an area in the Torah that contradicts science, we must always search for the deeper meaning of the text in order to overcome the problem. (IR 1, pp. 163–64)

We need a spiritual revolution in our understanding of the relationship between faith and science.

Fourteen: Liberal and Progressive Values

Today more than ever we see that fundamentalist religion is opposed to liberal and progressive values. This is true whether we look at Judaism, Christianity, Islam, or any other religion. Fundamentalism is based on the principle that all truth exists in the past – that God has already revealed to the prophet all the truth of existence. In sharp contrast, liberal thinkers assume that knowledge and morality progress as we move forward into the future. So where is truth to be found? In the past or in the future? In fundamentalism or in liberalism?

According to Rav Kook, in order to solve this issue, we must redefine what we mean when we say "divine revelation." For Rav Kook, divine revelation is not only something that happened once upon a time, but something that is happening at all times. In other words, in every generation God reveals His wisdom more and more; each generation builds on the last generation's understanding of God and truth.

And thus, according to Rav Kook, we have no need to fear liberal and progressive values. Religious truth evolves just as liberal truth does. In fact, according to the Gemara (*Menachot* 29b), Rabbi Akiva understands elements of God's will more than Moshe Rabeinu does.

This is not because Rabbi Akiva is objectively smarter than Moshe, but because Rabbi Akiva is building off the divine truth that Moshe Rabbeinu has already revealed. Indeed, this is one of Rav Kook's main insights into understanding history: that as we progress further in history, mankind uncovers more and more of God's truth. History is His-story.

On the other hand, Rav Kook believed that there is a major danger in liberalism: in its desire to progress, it tends to throw away the good qualities of the past. And therefore, in Rav Kook's eyes, instead of religion rejecting progressive values, it must help the world express these new ideas in the most sophisticated and mature way.

> Corresponding to the degree to which it has already been refined, liberalism is certain to spread, and anarchy will find its place. And when tradition and religion come, even in their most sophisticated form, to conquer this refined portion, they will not succeed. Instead, religion needs to encourage the spirit of man in the refined elements that it has already reached, and to refocus its attention toward those elements of the spirit, intelligence, and desire of mankind that are yet to be grounded, and are still standing in their state of corruption, like in ancient days. (OK 2, pp. 544–46, SK 1:109)

We need a spiritual revolution in our understanding of and relationship to liberal and progressive values.

Fifteen: Relationship to Other Religions

There are two main ways religious people relate to other religions:

(1) Exclusive religion. Those who see religion as exclusive argue that their religion and not anyone else's is the exclusive source for absolute truth in the world. They feel that in order to justify their beliefs, they must disprove and find fault in other religions.

(2) Pluralistic religion. Those who see religion as pluralistic explain

that all religions contain similar truths, and that the choice of which particular religion to follow is not a question of truth, but one of personal preference.

Yet Rav Kook's understanding of the Torah caused him to reject the overconfidence of the first category as well as the bland and mediocre neutrality of the second. Instead, Rav Kook believes that Judaism asks us to follow a third path:

(3) Inclusive religion. Those who see religion as inclusive believe that while their own religion has the most truth, elements of truth exist in other religions. In Rav Kook's eyes, there is absolutely no contradiction between saying that Judaism is the deepest and most beautiful manifestation of God's will and at the same time being humble enough to acknowledge wisdom in other religions.

Rav Kook, just like the Rambam in the 1100s, was humble enough to say that one can be loyal to one's own tradition while simultaneously being able to learn wisdom from other traditions.

> **The treasure of wisdom is secretly buried within the Jewish people. However, in order to unify the entire world together with it, the nation must be flawed and deficient in certain wisdoms. Therefore, the Jewish people must be open to being influenced. (O, "Yisrael" 5:2.3)**

We need a spiritual revolution in our understanding of and relationship to the other religions.

Sixteen: Animal Rights and Vegetarianism

Despite the overwhelming evidence in Jewish law that supports sensitivity to animals,[2] many Jews continue to assume that animal

---

2. Jewish law mandates animal slaughter done in the least painful way, not killing a bird in front of its mother, covering the blood of a dead animal, feeding one's pet before feeding oneself, and so on.

rights are New Age, liberal values that are foreign to the very essence of Judaism.

Rav Kook asks us to return to what he believes is an authentic Jewish attitude toward animals: that if God is the Creator of all creatures, then developing a concern for animals is a religious and spiritual value. In fact, anyone who is familiar with basic Jewish law knows that *tza'ar ba'alei chayim* (causing unnecessary suffering to animals) is biblically prohibited. Rav Kook, like other commentaries on the Torah,[3] brings the story of Adam and Chava in Gan Eden to prove that the original diet of humankind was vegetarianism; it was only after the flood of Noach that God permitted eating meat as a consolation.

Rav Kook says that as long as a person eats meat for the sake of being healthy, it is considered a mitzvah and a way of serving God. Nevertheless, based on biblical, rabbinical, and kabbalistic sources, Rav Kook believes that eating animals must be seen as a compromise and not an ideal. As humankind get closer to the times of the Mashiach, and moral sensitivity evolves, Rav Kook believes that eventually, all people will become so concerned about the suffering of life that they will naturally become vegetarians.

To be sure, Rav Kook did not think that everyone must give up eating meat in a sudden way. Rather, he believed it would come about as a natural spiritual and ethical development within humanity. It is Rav Kook's opinion that many Jewish laws, such as *shechitah* (kosher slaughter), covering the blood, and shooing away the mother bird, are there in order to train us to be more sensitive to animals, and eventually prepare us for a time when we will no longer desire to eat animals.

Amazingly, history has already proved much of what Rav Kook said as right; we see today more and more young people choosing to become vegetarians of their own volition.

---

3. See Rashi, Ibn Ezra, Ramban, Or Hachayim, and the majority of commentaries on the verses in Bereishit 1:29 and 9:3.

> At the end of days, there will be an inner thirst within humankind to do acts of righteousness. One will desire to pour out a spirit of kindness onto others, but none who need it will be found. Humanity will already be living a life of true happiness and success physically, ethically, and intellectually. At that time, humankind will turn to its lower brothers, the mute and downtrodden animals. Mankind will use its treasure of wisdom and experience to help teach and improve animals according to their abilities in physical, intellectual, ethical, and spiritual realms. (CT)

We need a spiritual revolution in our understanding of and relationship to animals.

Seventeen: Rav Kook's Own Inner World

On a personal level, even though Rav Kook died many years before I was born, he is easily the most influential person I have ever come across in my life. The way I trust my intuition, the way I love the Jewish people, the way I feel a spiritual obligation to care for the needs of all humanity, even the way I eat (I am a vegetarian) has been influenced and inspired by Rav Kook. Having a powerful role model has truly transformed my life.

On the other hand, I am aware of the danger of having a powerful role model; we can end up worshipping and blindly obeying those people we look up to. In our sincere desire to follow an exemplary person, we risk losing our own self and our own voice.

But how can we curb the tendency to worship our role models? What can we do to prevent our own personalities and understanding from being ignored in the face of theirs?

Perhaps this is Rav Kook's greatest spiritual revolution: he tells us about his highest spiritual achievements as well as his deepest struggles; he opens the door to both his most courageous moments as well as his greatest mistakes. In short, Rav Kook encourages us to witness both his angelic and human self. By doing this, he prevents us from passively worshiping him as a perfect idol, and instead asks us to use his passion for growth to inspire us on our own very personal journeys.

True spiritual guides do not manipulate you and force you to believe what they believe, but instead, empower you by giving you the tools to be your deepest self. A teacher must not suppress your dreams, but help you express them most profoundly.

I remember one time asking a spiritual teacher of mine, Dr. Aviezer Cohen, what he thought was the most important lesson he had learned from studying Rav Kook's words. I will never forget his answer: "Rav Kook taught me that I can disagree with Rav Kook."

Listen to Rav Kook describe his own inner wars in order to inspire within us the courage to confront our own struggles:

> Whoever said that my soul is torn spoke well. Certainly, it is torn. It is impossible for us to imagine a human being whose soul is not torn. Only an inanimate object is whole. A human being is full of opposing desires, an inner war that rages inside constantly. A person's entire struggle is to unify the torn parts of his or her soul through a greater vision that includes everything. Only then will one move toward harmony. (C, p. 228)

We need a spiritual revolution in our understanding of and relationship to our role models.

A Personal Challenge from Rav Kook

Reading Rav Kook's words isn't like reading a normal book. Yes, it is true that you can find inspiration and wisdom. Yet there is something more. Many people have told me that when they study the writings of Rav Kook, it almost feels as if he is calling out to the reader, asking them to do something, trying to challenge them.

But what is he challenging his reader to do?

The individual soul has been forgotten, the nation is full of religious and secular fighting, and the world is falling apart due to hatred and indifference. Yet Rav Kook asks us to stop complaining about the negativities and problems of life:

> Pointing fingers at the sickness... will not bring strength and life, since this attitude is pessimistic by its very nature. (IR 2, p. 123)

Instead, this is Rav Kook's challenge to the true spiritual seeker:

> The purest *tzaddikim* (righteous individuals) do not complain about evil, but instead increase righteousness. They do not complain about atheism, but instead increase faith. They do not complain about ignorance, but instead increase wisdom. (AT 80)

May the spiritual revolution of Rav Kook be a personal challenge to us all.

Meet Rav Kook

Birth of a Child Prodigy

Rav Kook was born Avraham Yitzchak Hakohen Kook on September 7, 1865 (16 Elul 5625), in Griva, a suburb of Dvinsk in Latvia, to Rav Shlomo Zalman and Pera Zlata Kook. He was the eldest of eight children. From a very young age, Rav Kook was aware of the divisions within the Jewish world, because his parents came from two opposing sects. His father studied in the Talmud-focused Volozhin Yeshiva, firmly entrenched in the Lithuanian Mitnagdic approach that opposed Chasidut, while his mother was a descendant of Chabad, a Chasidic group. Rav Kook's parents would argue over what their talented son would become when he grew up; his mother would bless him to be a charismatic spiritual leader, while his father would bless him to be a *talmid chacham* (wise Torah scholar).[1] In fact, it is told that when Rav Kook was a young boy, someone actually confronted him about this contradiction:

> Isn't your father a Mitnaged, and your mother is from the house of Chasidim? What will you be?"
> The young Rav Kook responded, "I will be both of them!"[2]

---

1. Simcha Raz, *An Angel among Men: Impressions from the Life of Rav Avraham Yitzchak Hakohen Kook*, trans. Moshe D. Lichtman (Jerusalem: Urim, 2003), p. 56.
2. SR, p. 52.

As we shall see, Rav Kook spent much of his life trying to create a philosophy of inclusive spirituality that could combine seemingly contradictory worlds.

> **Whoever said that my soul is torn spoke well. Certainly, it is torn. It is impossible for us to imagine a human being whose soul is not torn.... A person's entire struggle is to unify the torn parts of his or her soul.**[3]

In Rav Kook's early years, he earned himself the reputation of an *ilui* (a child prodigy). His father took him out of school at the age of nine and sent him to Dvinsk for an intensive rabbinic apprenticeship with Rav Reuven Levin.[4] At the age of eighteen, Rav Kook began studying in the Volozhin Yeshiva. This famous Lithuanian religious institution was founded by Rabbi Chaim Volozhin, a student of the Vilna Gaon. Rav Kook's learning schedule was very intense; he would learn eighteen hours each day, covering sixty pages of Talmud in depth.[5] Rav Kook became close to the *rosh yeshiva*, Rabbi Naftali Tzvi Yehuda Berlin. This famous rabbi, known as the Netziv, once said of Rav Kook, "It was worthwhile establishing the Volozhin Yeshiva just to produce a student like him."[6]

On the outside, Rav Kook looked like the perfect student. On the inside, however, he felt uninterested in memorizing dry information and simply becoming an expert learner. He would later express this attitude as follows:

> **The great spiritual people discover within themselves a resistance to being an expert learner, since everything is already alive within**

---

3. C, p. 228.
4. Yehudah Mirsky, *Rav Kook: Mystic in a Time of Revolution* (New Haven: Yale University Press, 2014), p. 12.
5. Raz, *An Angel among Men*, p. 26.
6. Raz, *An Angel among Men*, p. 25.

them.... They must focus their time uncovering the depths of their own souls. (SK 2:172)

Rav Kook wanted Torah learning to be more than just receiving information; he yearned to go through some kind of an inner transformation while studying the text. Later on in his life, he would encourage his students to search out parts of the Torah that spoke to their unique spiritual personalities:

> If one feels inspired and holy in a specific area of learning, then one must constantly satisfy oneself from this deep pleasure that one's heart desires. As for me personally, I am filled with a powerful sense of divine satisfaction when I study mystical Torah. (SK 8:24)

After years of soul searching, Rav Kook reached the conclusion that while it is true that a person must become familiar with all areas of the Torah, each person must give special emphasis to the part of the Torah that speaks to him or her the most. Indeed, one of the main parts of Rav Kook's spiritual revolution was the realization that forcing people to follow religion in a way that doesn't resonate on a personal level may turn them off of religion all together.

> There are some who have left religion because in their learning and spiritual perfection, they betrayed their unique personalities. For example, one may be naturally talented in matters of *aggadah* (spiritual and philosophical texts) and be unsuited to constant immersion in matters of *halachah* (matters of law). (OT 9:6)

Rav Kook was not speaking from an abstract place; he was aware of his own passion and unique connection to matters of *aggadah* and spirituality.

> Within my soul I know that my ideas concerning *halachah*, while they may be accurate explanations, do not form a new path that stands out from books already written. On the other hand,

concerning the world of *aggadah*, philosophy, and mysticism, even though I have only invested a small amount of time in them, I can see that with the help of God, I have already found a unique path. In fact, I have not come across books that contain ideas at all similar. (MS, introduction)

And so, at the age of eighteen, Rav Kook started working on *Ein Aya*, a commentary on all the spiritual stories of the Gemara tractates *Berachot* and *Shabbat*. By investing so much time in *aggadah*, Rav Kook made sure he would not neglect his unique personality. The *rosh yeshiva*, the Netziv, recognized early on that Rav Kook had a special talent for helping people who struggled with spiritual matters. Therefore, whenever a student in the yeshiva was struggling with questions of faith, the Netziv would send him to talk to Rav Kook.[7]

An Introverted Leader

In 1885, at the age of twenty, Rav Kook married Batsheva. Her father was Rabbi Eliyahu David Rabinowitz-Teomim (the Aderet), the head rabbi of Ponevezh, and later the chief rabbi of Jerusalem. At this stage of Rav Kook's life, he was focused mainly on spiritual growth and studying Torah in private, away from the distractions of the community. However, at the young age of twenty-two, due to a combination of financial troubles and the encouragement of the famed Chofetz Chaim, Rav Kook entered the rabbinate.[8] Not long after, he was appointed rabbi of Zeimel in Lithuania. Let it be clear, the decision to spend his life involved in public matters was not an easy one for Rav Kook. He often felt that being a public figure allowed no time for his

---

7. SR, p. 70.
8. SR, p. 81; Mirsky, *Rav Kook*, pp. 17–18. Rav Kook had already received rabbinic ordination from the Aruch Hashulchan (Rav Yechiel Michel Epstein) at the young age of nineteen and a half.

own spiritual growth. Throughout his life, he would write letters to people expressing his struggle in being a rabbinical leader.

> **Matters of the rabbinate are contrary to my very personality and talents, and I honestly yearn to sit in the holy land of Israel without the burden of providing rabbinical rulings for the community. (IR 1, p. 89)**

Yet, despite Rav Kook's introverted personality, there existed within him a powerful drive to connect to all people and relieve them of their suffering. Later in his life, Rav Kook's love of people would motivate him to write the following:

> **Listen to me, my people. I am speaking to you from my soul, from the soul of my soul. I am connected to you by my very connection to life, and you are all connected to me.... Without you, I am nothing. (C, p. 199)**

One of the first things Rav Kook did as a Jewish leader was to establish *Ittur Soferim*, a small Torah newspaper, which included his own essays as well as articles from esteemed rabbis on important spiritual topics.[9] This was a way for Rav Kook to channel his spiritual passion toward the community. Yet, as he would discover about himself time and again throughout his life, his spiritual vision clashed with his lack of practicality. Due to lack of funds,[10] he managed to publish only two issues of this newspaper.

Tragically, in 1889, not long after Rav Kook became the rabbi of Zeimel, his wife Batsheva contracted a fatal disease and passed away at age twenty-two, leaving him with a one-and-a-half-year-old daughter

---

9. Raz, *An Angel among Men*, p. 27.
10. Some say that his wife's death was another contributing factor to stopping his newspaper, *Ittur Soferim*. Avinoam Rosenak, "The Death of His Lover and Attempt at Rehabilitation," in *Rav Avraham Yitzchak Kook* (Jerusalem: Merkaz Zalman Shazar, 2006).

named Freida Chanah.[11] Rav Kook struggled to deal with the pain of losing his wife: "I have been very broken and much time has passed with great pain and sadness in my heart."[12] He wrote poems about his suffering: "She lies in the grave, but is still alive. There is no end to the pain and agony... from the darkness of confusion... my soul was abandoned...."[13]

Some say that the tragic death of his young wife caused Rav Kook to search for answers in kabbalah and Jewish mysticism;[14] he soon developed a close relationship with the great kabbalist Rav Shlomo Elyashiv, author of *Leshem Shevo v'Achlamah*. Rav Kook would travel to his kabbalistic master's home from time to time to study the secrets of the Torah.[15]

Soon after this, Rav Kook married Raiza-Rivka Rabinowitz, the niece of the Aderet. They had three children together: Tzvi Yehuda, Esther Yael, and Batya-Miriam Ra'anan. At the age of thirty, Rav Kook moved with his family to Boisk, where he was appointed rabbi of the city. During this period, Rav Kook compiled his *derashot* (sermons) into a book called *Midbar Shur*, in which he began developing some of his most influential ideas of how Torah, Jewish nationalism, and universal transformation are deeply connected. An essential principle of Rav Kook's spiritual revolution was the belief that diverse goals could be combined to create a holistic vision for the Jewish people, as he wrote:

> **It is God's will that each individual have his or her own spiritual purpose... and through the power of the holy Torah... everyone will come together for one unified purpose.... So too, the ulti-**

---

11. Raz, *An Angel among Men*, p. 27.
12. Quoted in Yehudah Mirsky's wonderful biography *Rav Kook*, p. 21.
13. PR 1, pp. 81–82.
14. Rosenak, "The Death of His Lover and Attempt at Rehabilitation."
15. Raz, *An Angel among Men*, p. 26.

mate goal of the Jewish people is the spiritual transformation of the entire world. (MS, p. 115)

Aliyah Despite Opposition

Rav Kook's reputation spread throughout European Jewry during his service as the rabbi of Zeimel and Boisk. It wasn't long until prominent yeshivas, such as the Telz Yeshiva, attempted to convince Rav Kook to teach at their institutions.[16] Rav Kook surprised many admirers when, in 1904, at the age of thirty-nine, he accepted an offer to move to Israel and become the rabbi of Yaffo. Religious Zionists were puzzled by this decision, since Rav Kook had not been directly involved with the Zionist movement; but what was even more surprising was his decision to move to the city of Yaffo, which was known for being an extremely secular and anti-religious town.[17]

The greatest rabbis of Europe, including Rav Chaim Ozer Grodzinski of Vilna, tried to dissuade Rav Kook from going; even rabbis in Israel recommended that he not settle in the town of Yaffo. Many were afraid that Rav Kook would not be accepted by the two extremes of the city: the Old Yishuv (religious) and the New Yishuv (secular). Nevertheless, Rav Kook stubbornly stuck to his decision and ignored these warnings.

What was his motivation for moving to the controversial city of Yaffo?[18] It is difficult to give a concrete answer to this question; however, it seems that one possible answer is that Rav Kook was

---

16. Raz, *An Angel among Men*, p. 28.
17. Mirsky, *Rav Kook*, pp. 40–41.
18. Mirsky lists a number of possible motivations for Rav Kook to move to Israel: "The unquestioned sanctity of the Land of Israel and the biblical commandment to live in it, the opportunity to step onto a larger stage, the chance to be reunited with his still beloved former father-in-law, a sense of adventure, and the stirrings that in those same years were bringing to Palestine a tumultuous generation whose awakenings moved in him too." Mirsky, *Rav Kook*, pp. 41.

attracted to the opportunity to be involved with these more rebellious secular Zionist souls. Whereas most religious Jews were intimidated by such a rebellion against religion, Rav Kook identified with their sincerity and idealism. Indeed, it seems that throughout Rav Kook's life, his main goal was always to seek out the good within all people, unify opposite groups, and create an inclusive spiritual philosophy, an attitude he once expressed as follows:

> I love all people. I will never change this quality of mine. In every single person, I can find a good quality – literally in every one. (C, p. 191)

Optimistic Spirituality

On June 3, 1904, the founding father of Zionism, Theodore Herzl, died at the young age of forty-four. The newly appointed rabbi of Yaffo, Rav Kook, was asked to give a speech at a memorial service. The religious were against him speaking, since Herzl was the leader of the secular Zionists. On the other hand, the secular expected Rav Kook to speak, since Herzl was their hero. Craving to please both the religious and secular, Rav Kook decided to give a speech without explicitly mentioning the name of Herzl.[19] However, this did not resolve the problem. Both sides were left feeling disappointed.

Yet Rav Kook was not deterred, and he began working on his long-planned spiritual revolution. His educational goals included strengthening existing religious organizations (Tachkemoni, Shaarei Torah), as well as creating a new spiritual institution called HaYeshivah HaMercazit HaOlamit (the central universal yeshiva), which would train religious leaders to combine a passion for Torah with a love of the land of Israel. In addition, Rav Kook sent letters to his

---

19. See Rabbi Bezalel Naor's introduction to Rav Kook's unofficial eulogy of Herzl in his book *When God Becomes History: Historical Essays of Rabbi Avraham Isaac Hakohen Kook* (New York: Kodesh Press, 2016), pp. 21–60.

friends and students announcing the great need to create spiritual books that would translate the beauty of Judaism into a language the secular Zionists would understand.

> In order to attract the people of our generation, we must translate all of our holy writings – the principles and emotions of almost the entire Torah – into a modern language. (IR 2, pp. 226)

Rav Kook published two books of his own, *Eder Hayakar* (1905), and *Ikvei Hatzon* (1906).

In 1910, at the age of forty-five, Rav Kook made a courageous but controversial decision to use a halachic leniency called *heter mechirah* (permission to sell [the land]), which allowed the secular Zionists to work the land during the *shemittah* year (the Torah forbids working the land every seventh year). Rav Kook relied on previous rabbinical rulings introduced by Rabbi Shmuel Mohiliver and other respected rabbis that argued that the law does not apply when the national economy is at risk. Rav Kook wrote a book called *Shabbat Ha'aretz* (Resting the land), in which he tried to explain the halachic reasoning for his decision; nevertheless, many were not satisfied, and many turned on him.

Refusing to give up his optimism, in 1913, Rav Kook led a group of rabbis – including many of his religious opponents – on a *teshuvah* (spiritual growth) campaign. Together, they traveled all over Israel to the secular Zionist settlements in an attempt to unify the religious and the secular. The more Rav Kook witnessed with his own eyes secular Zionists literally dedicating their bodies to building the land of Israel, the more he developed an appreciation for the holiness of the human body. He would later write:

> The demand for physicality is enormous. We need healthy bodies. But we have been so focused on our souls that we have forgotten the holiness of the body. We have neglected our health and strength, and have forgotten that we possess holy bodies no less than we possess holy souls. (O, "Hatechiyah" 33)

Yet the other religious leaders were not as impressed by the secular Zionists as Rav Kook was, and his inclusive spirituality often frustrated them. Again and again, Rav Kook would learn the same hard lesson: in his attempt to please everyone, he would always end up offending someone. Nevertheless, it was part of Rav Kook's greatness that despite the religious and secular communities not always accepting his ways, he refused to give in to despair; his optimistic attitude always overcame pessimism.

> We need to develop a spiritual outlook that will not focus on the negativities in secular values, but instead concentrate on transforming them into a more spiritual and beautiful form. (SK 6:230)

Hope in Exile

Rav Kook was deeply in love with the spiritual atmosphere of the land of Israel, and he had no intention of leaving. However, in 1914 he was invited to speak at Agudat Yisrael's Knessiah Hagedolah (Great Assembly) in Frankfurt, Germany. After debating with his family and students whether or not he should leave Israel for an entire month, eventually he decided that he must go, since it was an incredible opportunity to help strengthen diaspora Jewry's love of the land of Israel. Shortly after Rav Kook arrived in Germany, World War I broke out, and all paths of transportation back to Israel were cut off. He was heartbroken; in letters to family and friends, Rav Kook wrote about his inner frustration:

> It is very difficult for me to endure this situation; I do not even know how long this will continue, due to the chaos of war. I only hope to God that He will not abandon me. (IR 2, p. 331)

While stuck in exile, Rav Kook wrote many of his most famous essays about the spiritual power of the land of Israel.

> Where can I get the joy of the land of Israel, the inner peace of the land of Israel?... God of mercy, please have compassion on me. Give me the merit to fully return to You; please return me to Your beautiful land. (C, p. 187)

What Rav Kook imagined would be a month-long trip to Germany ended up being a total of five long years in Europe. He spent one and a half years in Switzerland (a neutral territory during the war), where he fundraised for struggling institutions in Israel, as well as three and a half years in England, where he became the rabbi of the Machzike Hadath community in London. In 1917, Rav Kook campaigned for what would eventually be called the Balfour Declaration, whereby the British government officially stated that it favored "the establishment in Palestine of a national home for the Jewish people."[20]

Toward the end of his time in Europe, Rav Kook tried to establish an alternative to the existing religious Zionist movement Mizrachi. He called his new movement Degel Yerushalayim (the flag of Jerusalem), and through it, he hoped to attract the more religious sects toward Zionism. He sent out letters all over the world and announced the creation of his new movement:

> Rabbis, congregations and individuals, please answer our call... and help us create... the Flag of Jerusalem. (IR 3, p. 148)

In this public letter, he explained that the word *Zion* represents the physical revolution, while the word *Jerusalem* represents the spiritual revolution. According to Rav Kook, the "Flag of Zionism" would focus on building the body of the Jewish people, while the "Flag of Jerusalem" would concentrate on reviving the soul of the Jewish people. Rather than acting as enemies, Zion and Jerusalem would be partners in building up the Jewish people in its new yet ancient

---

20. See "Balfour Declaration 1917," Yale Law School Documents in Law, History and Diplomacy, http://avalon.law.yale.edu/20th_century/balfour.asp.

land. However, his idealistic vision once again clashed with his lack of practical abilities, and his new movement, the Flag of Jerusalem, never came about.

During these five years in exile, Rav Kook's wife and son were with him, but he intensely missed his three daughters and his parents, who were living in Israel at the time.[21] He wrote to his son-in-law in Israel:

> **Have you seen my children at home?... Perhaps you have some time to go speak with my little girl, Esther Yael? She is wise beyond her years. (IR 2, p. 330)**

We can hear in these words the longing and pain that Rav Kook experienced from being away from his loved ones for so long.

While most people would have considered these five years an extremely productive time period for Rav Kook, in his own eyes, creating social change without going through inner transformation of his own felt empty. Rav Kook felt that he had no time for his own thoughts. "Because of the many obligations... I am forced to write only small paragraphs."[22] Rav Kook's introverted personality was overwhelmed by the social responsibilities of being a public figure; he craved personal time:

> **If my situation in the diaspora was free of all these little jobs, I would be excited to work on certain spiritual tasks... to actualize things that I already began in the land of Israel. (IR 3, p. 103)**

Yet here again we see Rav Kook's inner power: despite his struggle of being away from family and the severe lack of personal time, he never gave in to despair. He stubbornly searched out a way to be positive and make peace with his situation.

> **Even though I am stuck in exile; even though I suffer great pain – both physical and spiritual – the kindness of God will not**

---

21. I want to thank Professor Yehudah Mirsky for helping me clarify this.
22. IR 3, p. 97.

abandon me. I need to elevate myself to a higher freedom, to that which I had with me in the land of Israel. (C, p. 186)

Returning to Israel

At the end of World War I, Rav Kook was offered the position of chief rabbi of Jerusalem. Although at first, he did not want to abandon his beloved followers in the city of Yaffo, the overwhelming support of rabbis and leaders in Israel opened his eyes to how influential he could be in this new role. Rav Kook received letters imploring him to come to Jerusalem and be their spiritual leader:

> Our great Rabbi! . . . We say this with honesty and purity that we can see the throne of the Jerusalem rabbinate standing and waiting for your arrival to the holy city for you to sit on it. There is no person in the entire land except for you who can do this holy work, for the benefit of building up the broken and destroyed Jerusalem. (IR 3, p. 302)

And so, in 1920, at the age of fifty-five, Rav Kook moved to Jerusalem and became its chief rabbi.

To be sure, Rav Kook's return to Israel was mixed with both joy and sadness. After years of waiting to come back to be with his family, he suffered a devastating tragedy soon after being reunited with them: in 1919, his twelve-year-old daughter, Esther Yael, fell down a flight of stairs at their home in Jerusalem, broke her neck, and died immediately. Rav Kook was brokenhearted; this was the second time a close member of his family had died at a very young age (his first wife was twenty-two when she passed away). Some witnesses said that Rav Kook was visibly devastated by the death of his beloved daughter; he simply could not be consoled by anyone's words.[23] How much

---

23. In my own conversations with Rabbi Yochanan Fried, chairman of Beit HaRav Kook and a student of Rav Kook's son, I was told about the intense pain Rav Kook experienced due to his daughter's death.

sadness could Rav Kook have been experiencing at such a moment? For years he had dreamed of reuniting with his little girl, and now she was gone forever. Not long after her death, Rav Kook wrote the following letter to a friend:

> **You must already have heard about the terrible and shocking tragedy that happened to us immediately as we returned to the holy land. Our precious daughter and beautiful girl was taken from us in the most terrifying and sudden way; it has left an extremely deep wound in our souls. (IR 4, p. 48)**

And yet, after spending a full thirty years pondering the meaning of his first wife's death, this time Rav Kook stubbornly searched for a positive way of reacting to this tragic event. During shivah (the first week of mourning), someone overheard Rav Kook whisper to himself, "Instead of crying bitterly over the death of our daughter, we should remember gratefully that God gave her to us for twelve years to gladden our hearts."[24]

Rav Kook is sometimes criticized for having a naïve and overly optimistic philosophy toward life. The argument goes that if he had witnessed the horrors of the Holocaust, he wouldn't have had such a positive attitude toward everything. Yet this argument is mistaken since it does not take into account how much Rav Kook experienced suffering in his own life – he lost his first wife at a young age, spent World War I in Europe, and saw the death of his twelve-year-old daughter after spending five years dreaming of reuniting with her. Instead, we must conclude from this that Rav Kook was not naïve about the hardships of life; he stubbornly searched for an optimistic spiritual philosophy that enabled him to deal with the pain in a positive and meaningful way.[25]

---

24. Raz, *An Angel among Men*, p. 323.
25. Rabbi Dr. Neriya Gutal, head of Michlelet Orot, wrote an important article analyzing how Rav Kook reacted to his daughter's tragic death. His main argument

Major Innovations

In 1921, soon after moving to Jerusalem, Rav Kook helped to establish a central rabbinate recognized by the British government that represented all the major Jewish communities of the Land of Israel. Not long after, this council appointed Rav Kook as the chief Ashkenazic rabbi of Israel. Rav Kook did not like the idea of people giving him so much honor, and would famously sign his letters "a servant to a holy people on a holy land." Indeed, rather than use his authoritative position to receive honor, he took full advantage of his connections in order to help Soviet Jews immigrate to Israel, as well as to help any organizations or people struggling with financial issues. Rav Kook publicly invited anyone who needed his help to come speak to him in his home at any time of the day.

While Rav Kook spent much of his time focused on public responsibilities, whenever he had free time, he would write down his thoughts in a diary. Rav Kook dreamed of publishing his own writings as a way of inspiring a spiritual revolution within the Jewish people.

> I am always fighting this inner battle: a powerful spirit is pushing me to speak about *teshuvah* (spiritual growth). All of my thoughts are focused on it.... I must help our generation understand its depth and guide them to actualize it in our individual and collective lives.[26]

Rav Charlap, one of Rav Kook's closest students, once told Rav Kook that if he really wanted his spiritual ideas to be accepted by the religious world, he must first write an important halachic book in order to win their approval. To his student's surprise, Rav Kook

---

is that Rav Kook used the pain to inspire himself to dedicate his life to the Jewish people. "The Death of a Daughter: Communal Growth from a Personal Tragedy in the Life of Rav Kook" [Hebrew], https://orot.ac.il/sites/default/files/6-5_0.pdf.
26. OTs, introduction.

replied, "Ideas must be inspired organically.... If the Rambam had written *Yad Hachazakah* [his halachic book] just in order that *Guide for the Perplexed* [his philosophical book] be accepted, he would not have succeeded."[27] Rav Kook refused to be a fake. Again and again, he tried to show his students a path of spirituality that was filled with authenticity and self-belief.

Over the next few years, with the help of his son and student Rav Tzvi Yehuda – who would be the one to transform many of his father's powerful visions into a practical movement – Rav Kook published a number of his own writings: *Orot* (1921), on spiritual Zionism; *Igrot Hare'iyah* (1925), a collection of letters; and *Orot Hateshuvah* (1925), on spiritual growth (*teshuvah*). Tzvi Yehuda told the following powerful story about trying to remove a controversial paragraph on holy exercise when editing his father's books:

> **When I was editing his holy books, I said to him, "Maybe we should remove this paragraph on holy exercise?" My father rebuked me and said, "This is not coming from a fear of God, but from a fear of people. This is a weakness toward [my] holy words, which are inspired by the Divine." He rebuked me and didn't let me remove it. And thus, it remained in the book.**[28]

In 1924, Rav Kook actualized his dream of creating a spiritual center, a yeshiva in Jerusalem for the entire Jewish people. It was called HaYeshivah HaMercazit HaOlamit (today called Mercaz HaRav). The curriculum Rav Kook prepared for the yeshiva was very holistic: Talmud, *halachah*, Chasidut, philosophy, kabbalah, Jewish history,

---

27. SR, p. 196.
28. To read more about this story and Rav Kook's students' attempts and successes in censoring many of his writings, see "The Circle of Rav Kook and the Editing of His Writings" by Meira Mintz (Bar-Ilan University, October 2008). In this comprehensive doctoral thesis, Mintz argues that Rav Kook's students both changed and deleted some of his words in order to emphasize national ideas, while deemphasizing individual, universal, and kabbalistic ideas.

Hebrew, and even academic scholarship.[29] In addition, Rav Kook believed it was very important for his students to understand how ancient Talmudic debates directly influence modern halachic decisions.

As a result, Rav Kook spent close to sixteen years working on his magnum opus, *Halachah Berurah* – a commentary on the Babylonian and Jerusalem Talmuds presenting the opinions of the Rambam and *Shulchan Aruch* at the bottom of each page. This was a massive undertaking, especially considering Rav Kook's main passion was Jewish philosophy and mysticism, and not Jewish law. While working on this enormous halachic project, Rav Kook once commented:

> When the philosopher Kant wanted to rest a bit from his philosophical pursuits, he would study geography, saying, "Since I am an abstract thinker, I feel relaxed and regenerated when I explore concrete matters, such as mountains, rivers, cities, and villages." The same is true of me. I am an intellectual and emotional person by nature. So, when I wish to rest a bit, I delve into *halachah*. Then I feel my feet standing on solid ground. (Raz, *An Angel among Men*, p. 177)

Rav Kook was a shining example of his own religious philosophy that when one is given the time to find a personal and unique connection to Judaism, one eventually finds the strength to connect to both dimensions of the Torah – spirituality and *halachah*. In order to give advice to others, Rav Kook would often use the lessons he had learned from his own personal struggles.

> When I was young, I also was not excited to study *halachah*. My heart was drawn after *aggadah*. However, by studying *aggadah*, I came to study *halachah*. I suggest you teach your son *aggadah*, and as a result, he will also come to study *halachah*. (SR, p. 180)

---

29. MaR, pp. 62–65.

Indeed, Rav Kook would eventually go on to write great books on both *halachah* and *aggadah*. Rav Kook spent much of his life writing *Ein Aya*, a commentary on all the *aggadot* (spiritual stories) in Gemara tractates *Berachot* and *Shabbat*.

Ultimately, the main goal of Rav Kook's yeshiva was to create a new type of religious person: one who combined a passion for spiritual growth, a love for one's nation, and a deep concern for universal transformation.

> And then there is one who rises up with all these songs together. Each gives its voice. Each plays its melody: the song of the soul, the song of the nation, the song of humanity, and the song of existence. All harmonize within the ideal human being at every moment and at all times. (OK 2, pp. 444–45)

Struggles and Accomplishments

In 1924, Rav Kook traveled to America with a group of esteemed rabbis to raise funds for Torah institutions in Israel. Although Rav Kook attracted hundreds and thousands of people to hear him talk, impressing them with his charismatic spiritual personality, nevertheless, his lack of practicality prevented him from attaining the funds needed. This was something Rav Kook struggled with his entire life: he was able to come up with the most inspirational visions, yet without his son Rav Tzvi Yehuda's practical planning, Rav Kook often felt helpless.

> I hope it is clear, concerning any practical matters that I refer to, that I do not desire to accept any responsibility. As you know, I am only able to deal with the spirit of our holy land and the revival of our holy people upon it. But I do not deal in details. I would be very happy if through my words of inspiration, practical matters would take care of themselves. (IR 2, p. 50)

In 1925, after returning from his inspirational yet unsuccessful fundraising trip in America, Rav Kook participated in the opening ceremony of the Hebrew University in Jerusalem. Many religious zealots were angry that Rav Kook would involve himself with such a secular institution, let alone give a speech there. Nevertheless, this was always Rav Kook's way: not to complain and focus on the negative elements of people or institutions, but to stubbornly seek out the good within everything.

> **The highest type of thinking... never rejects any idea in the world. Instead, it purifies it and guides it toward the good. (SK 1:480)**

While it is true that Rav Kook didn't totally agree with everything the university taught – specifically when it came to religious studies – he believed it was extremely important to communicate an inclusive voice of Torah and Jewish spirituality. Two years previously, when Albert Einstein visited Israel in 1923, Rav Kook sent him a letter in order to arrange a meeting: "To the honorable giant among the wise men of the world, Professor Albert Einstein. Shalom!... I would be delighted to receive his honorable presence... for him to arrange a time and place with me at his convenience..." (IR 4, p. 150). According to eyewitnesses, Rav Kook showed Einstein kabbalistic sources for the Theory of Relativity. Einstein was "amazed that a rabbi in the Jewish people had such a deep understanding of his scientific investigations" and said that Rav Kook's "knowledge contained something that many of the greatest scientists are unable to understand."[30]

Many of Israeli's greatest writers and poets, such as Shai Agnon and Nachman Bialik, were so inspired by Rav Kook's warmth and spiritual openness that they would often visit his home in Jerusalem to discuss topics of spirituality and personal meaning. When Shai Agnon was once asked why he never wrote a novel based on Rav Kook, Agnon replied, "I could never do him justice." Years earlier, when the

---

30. Quoted in *Zohar Elyon* (Jerusalem: Or Ha'orot 2011), p. 75. See also M.J. Zuriel, ed., *Otzrot Hare'iyah* (Sha'alvim: Yeshivat Sha'alvim, 1988), vol. 1, p. 20. I would like to thank Rabbi Ari Shvat for helping me gather these sources and clarify what really happened with Rav Kook and Einstein.

Bezalel Academy of Arts and Design was founded in 1906, Rav Kook was one of the very few Orthodox rabbis to publicly support this institution. Boris Schatz (1866–1932), the founder and dean of the school, was so appreciative of Rav Kook's support that he gave him a tapestry as a gift. Rav Kook immediately hung it on the wall in the main room of his house for all to see. It remains there to this day.[31]

Rav Kook was not afraid of any external authority. Not only was he willing to stand up to closed-minded religious thinking, he also had the courage to fight the British for basic Jewish rights. In 1928, British officers interrupted a Yom Kippur service at the Kotel;[32] in 1929, Arab rioters murdered 130 Jews throughout Israel with rumors of British incitement; and in 1930, the British government proclaimed its second White Paper, preventing Jewish immigration to Israel. Rav Kook risked his reputation with the British when he publicized a powerful protest statement:

> **Let everyone in the world know that it was not some gentile kingdom that gave us... the holy land. Rather, the Holy One of Israel, God of the entire world... gave us the holy land as an eternal inheritance... and if a government... betrays its mission... we can be sure that they will not succeed in destroying God's eternal plan.**[33]

By the end of Rav Kook's life, his quest for truth became so essential to who he was that he was even willing to damage his relationship with his beloved secular Zionist admirers in order to stand up for divine justice. In 1933, Avraham Stavsky, a member of the right-wing Zionists' Revisionist sect, was sentenced to death due to accusations

---

31. To read more about this story and many other relationships Rav Kook had with novelists, artists, and poets, see Raz, *An Angel among Men*, pp. 383–412.
32. M. Kolinsky and Willy Jou, *Law, Order and Riots in Mandatory Palestine, 1928–35* (London: MacMillan, 1993), 35. See also Raz, *An Angel among Men*, pp. 45, 206–23.
33. Raz, *An Angel among Men*, p. 47.

that he had murdered Chaim Arlosoroff of the left-wing Zionists' Labor sect. There was no strong evidence to prove that Stavsky was guilty, and a massive argument broke out between the left-wing and right-wing Jews of Israel. After initial silence regarding the issue, Rav Kook eventually decided that it was a spiritual and moral obligation to prevent Stavsky's death. In an open letter to the public, he wrote:

> We must not stand indifferent! Any Jew or gentile who has a spark of God in his heart must protest this sin of spilling innocent and righteous blood. We must do whatever we can to stop this injustice and save the innocent victim, Avraham Stavsky.[34]

A Humble Hero

Throughout Rav Kook's diaries, we find him struggling with the question of when prophecy will return to the Jewish people.

> The sprouts of prophecy are growing, *bnei nevi'im* (the descendants of prophets) are awakening, and the spirit of prophecy is rising in Israel. (SK 4:17)

While for most people, such questions are merely theoretical, for Rav Kook, it was a personal dilemma. When he was forced to leave Israel and mistakenly got stuck in Europe for five years, he pondered how it was possible that the spiritual inspiration he had received in Israel was still with him in exile.

> The experience of *ruach hakodesh* (divine inspiration) that happens in the land of Israel is a permanent event, even if a person is forced out of Israel due to a mistake or an urgent necessity, just as prophecy that was encountered in the land of Israel did not discontinue even outside Israel. (O, "Eretz Yisrael" 6)

---

34. Raz, *An Angel among Men*, p. 227.

Was it possible, Rav Kook thought to himself, that he had received prophecy? Afraid to tell anyone his inner thoughts and emotions, he wrote them down in a dairy entry one day:

> I listen and I hear from the depths of my soul, from among the feelings of my heart, the voice of God calling. I experience a great trembling; have I so descended as to become a *navi sheker* (false prophet), to say God sent me when the word of God has not been revealed to me? Yet I feel my soul yearning as the growth of prophecy increases. (SK 4:17)

While we may never know what conclusion he reached, it seems that this question of prophecy was Rav Kook's way of struggling with the value and authority of his own thoughts, emotions, and intuitions. Earlier on in his life, Rav Kook tried to please everyone, both religious and secular. He wanted to convince the religious that he was just as religious as them, while at the same time to persuade the secular that he was just as free and open-minded as them. Yet rather than win both sides' approval, Rav Kook often caused each side to feel betrayed and even resentful. He was frustrated that he couldn't please everyone. And thus, over many years of spiritual development, he eventually reached the conclusion that he no longer needed to bow down to external pressure, whether religious or secular.

> If I must be a person who argues with the entire world, because my soul is so drawn to truth that it cannot bear any type of lie, then it is impossible for me to be anyone else. I need to actualize the principles of truth that are hidden deep within my spirit, without any considerations of whether the world agrees with me. This is the way of a seeker of truth who is inspired by a higher strength. (C, p. 158)

This was one of the insights that Rav Kook discovered about himself by the end of his life: the more deeply he believed in God, the more he must trust in his own intuition. Nothing would hold him back from standing up for what he believed was true.

> I need to speak a lot about myself; matters of my essence must become very clear to me. Through understanding myself I will understand everything – the world, life – until I reach the source of life. (SK 7:189)

Did Rav Kook think his ideas of inclusive spirituality were prophetic? We are not sure. Yet what is certain is that Rav Kook believed that his own ideas were worth fighting for.

Throughout Rav Kook's life, he was depicted by his followers as a perfect saint, with perfect character traits, perfect learning abilities, and perfect faith in God. Indeed, since Rav Kook's death, much has been written about his impressive intellectual ability to synthesize philosophy and mysticism,[35] his great love of Zionism,[36] and his pursuit of prophetic and mystical experiences.[37]

Yet, the more we delve into Rav Kook's own writings, the more we discover a man who went out of his way to describe his own struggles, imperfections, and vulnerabilities.[38]

> I have to confess that I am not capable of writing clearly.... I want to pour out my soul in whatever form it takes. And I am

---

35. Benjamin Ish-Shalom, *Rav Avraham Itzhak HaCohen Kook: Between Rationalism and Mysticism* (Albany: SUNY Press, 1993); Yoel Bin-Nun, "The Double Source of Human Inspiration and Authority in the Philosophy of Rav Kook" (Hebrew University of Jerusalem, 2009).
36. See Zvi Yaron, *The Philosophy of Rav Kook* (Jerusalem: Eliner Library, 1992), for a detailed explanation of Rav Kook's loving relationship with secular Zionists.
37. Smadar Cherlow, *Tzaddiq Yesod Olam: Rabbi Kook's Secret Mission and Mystical Experience* (Ramat Gan: Bar-Ilan Press, 2013).
38. To read a more in-depth analysis of this important topic, see my essay "Rav Kook's Educational Goal of Describing His Own Imperfections," submitted to Herzog Academic College in 2017 as an undergraduate paper.

> not so worried about the editing demands, which you know are difficult for me. (IR 1, p. 267)

Rav Kook wanted his students to know that although he might be an inspirational leader, he wasn't perfect; he too struggled with his spiritual learning and relationship with people. "I force myself to learn, act, socialize; to do different obligations, until no one thought ever gets the opportunity to become complete and mature."[39]

And while Rav Kook believed that it was an extremely valuable tool to have a spiritual role model, throughout his writings he tried to warn his students about the dangers of worshipping a role model.

> **One must be very careful. For if one makes a mistake with a righteous person, and becomes completely attached to him to the point of also attaching to his flaws, these flaws will sometimes express themselves far more negatively in the loyal follower than they did in the leader himself. (O, "Orot Yisrael" 3:3)**

In many of his writings, Rav Kook hints to his students not to worship him. He writes that he too has flaws,[40] and that the angelic persona that the public gave him is not completely honest. It seems that one of Rav Kook's main educational goals as a *tzaddik*, rabbi, and leader was to inspire his students without them worshipping him. He strived to motivate them to aspire to great heights of spirituality without them passively relying on him and to show the beauty in being human and vulnerable.

> **I am certain that the world does not understand my value, the depth of my intellect, and the breadth of my thoughts. In the same way, they do not understand my faults, my deficiencies, my imperfections, and the flaws of my mind. (C, p. 162)**

---

39. C, p. 18.
40. See Yoel Bin-Nun's doctoral thesis "The Double Source of Human Inspiration and Authority in the Philosophy of Rav A.I.H. Kook," in which he explains that Rav Kook's statement that even *tzaddikim* have flaws is actually referring to himself.

By the end of his life, Rav Kook already saw the beginnings of students who wanted to create a movement out of him, to turn him into a perfect idol. Yet over and over again, Rav Kook told people that to be a true follower of his ideas was not to turn him into a saint, but to use his inspiration to contribute to the world.

> Do not create "Kookniks" for me. Any Jew who is dedicated to helping the Torah and Judaism is one of us. (*Nefesh Hare'iyah l'Shloshah b'Elul* 1:46)

Death and Making Peace with His Life

In 1935, Rav Kook turned seventy, and he was awarded the title of honorary citizen by the Tel Aviv municipality. Usually Rav Kook didn't like it when people gave him honor, preferring to give honor to other people instead. Nonetheless, he said that this specific title he would proudly accept, since it was for honorary citizenship of the first modern Jewish city. Yet again, Rav Kook found a way to communicate to the secular Zionists an inclusive spirituality that legitimized their values; rather than rejecting this title as something superficial, he recognized the good quality within it.

A few months later, Rav Kook began feeling very sick and was soon diagnosed with cancer. Due to the severe pain he was suffering, Rav Kook's doctor advised him to move to a sanatorium outside the city. Before leaving, Rav Kook asked to be driven all around Jerusalem; he sensed it might be his last time. Rav Kook's relationship to the land of Israel had developed into something deeply personal; he didn't see it as some external possession, but something that was intrinsically connected to who he was.

> The land of Israel is not just some external object, some material possession of the nation. Nor is it just some tool to achieve unity and strengthen our physical and even spiritual existence. Rather, the essence of the land of Israel is tied to the very life of the Jewish people. (O, "Eretz Yisrael" 1)

Despite his family's effort to get him to rest as much as possible, Rav Kook stubbornly spent the last few months of his life focused on his two main loves: spirituality and caring for people. Every spare second he had, Rav Kook was either studying Torah, praying, or receiving visitors in order to help them with their problems. It seems that up until the very end of his life, Rav Kook was struggling with his lifelong dilemma of how to balance caring for one's own spiritual growth while helping the community.

On one of the last Yom Kippurs of his life, Rav Kook told Rav Charlap, one of his closest students, that he had finally reached inner peace regarding those who opposed him.

> **You see, I have always tried to completely forgive all those who persecute me, even if they do not regret their actions, and even if they intend on attacking me again in the future. However, this Yom Kippur, I actually succeeded!** (Raz, *An Angel among Men*, p. 447)

On September 1, 1935 (3 Elul 5695), after a short but intense struggle with cancer, Rav Kook passed away. The Jewish people fell into national mourning. The newspaper heading read: "The Jews of the land of Israel have been orphaned: Rav Avraham Yitzchak Hakohen Kook is no longer."[41] And while Rav Kook himself may be no longer living, the spiritual revolution that he wrote about in his books, diaries, and letters is still with us. People are still searching for a way of life that will connect them to their souls, the Jewish people is still seeking an inclusive spirituality that will unite religious and secular, and the world is still dreaming of a time when each person will see the good in everyone. And therefore, in a very profound way, Rav Kook's ideas are still waiting for the courageous soul to turn them into a reality.

---

41. Raz, *An Angel among Men*, p. 53.

Any person whose heart is filled with courage, whose pen is filled with strength, and whose soul is filled with the spirit of God is being called to march out into the streets and cry out loud, "Let there be light!" (IR 2, p. 123)

Acknowledgments

I WOULD LIKE TO THANK ALL OF MY STUDENTS OVER THE PAST years who have challenged me to clarify Rav Kook's words and helped remind me why his words have so much to teach us. I would like to thank Rabbi Dr. Yoel Bin-Nun, Dr. Baruch Kahana, and Rabbi David Aaron, the three main teachers who introduced me to the many faces of Rav Kook. In particular, it was Rabbi Bin-Nun's doctoral thesis, "The Double Source of Human Inspiration and Authority in the Philosophy of Rav Kook," that opened my eyes to the sophisticated outlook needed to fully understand the wisdom of Rav Kook. I wish to thank Rabbi Dr. Yehudah Mirsky, Rabbi Ari Shvat, and Rabbi Levi Morrow for many insightful emails and conversations that have helped clarify certain topics about Rav Kook.

Thank you to Bnei Akiva, and specifically Nati Recht, for giving me the opportunity to teach this book to such diverse students from all around the world. Thank you to my older brother Jacob Schwartz for investing so much of his time in creating an aesthetically engaging front cover, and to my younger brother Zac Schwartz, for studying Rav Kook with me in *chavruta* over the years. Thank you to Maya Ben-Shushan, for helping me publicize the book, as well as for being my first *talmid-chaver* (student-friend) to really study this book in depth. Thank you to Leor Holzer and Michael Pomeranz, for believing in this book so much, as well as creating bookstores that embody Rav Kook's inclusive spirituality where all types of people are welcome.

Thank you to Gefen Publishing House in general, and Ilan Greenfield, Kezia Raffel Pride, Lynn Douek, and Emily Wind in particular, for their professionalism and generosity.

I thank my extraordinary parents, Andrew Schwartz and Vicki Moliver Schwartz, for their never-ending love and support. Tzofia Leah and Yael Hadar, my two gorgeous daughters, this book is my gift to you; I only hope that Rav Kook's wisdom will illuminate your lives as much as it has mine.

And finally, I want to thank Hashem for leading me to Rav Kook, a role model who has truly changed my life by teaching me to care for my soul, my people, and the entire world.

About the Author

RABBI ARI ZE'EV SCHWARTZ IS THE COFOUNDER AND DEAN OF the Society of Independent Spirituality, an English-speaking learning center in Jerusalem that combines Jewish spirituality and Zionism. Rabbi Schwartz is originally from Sydney, Australia, and studied at the University of New South Wales majoring in music and film before coming to Jerusalem, where he studied for eight years in several yeshivot in the Old City. Rabbi Schwartz received his rabbinical ordination at the Shehebar Sephardic Center in Jerusalem under Rabbi Yaakov Peretz, has a B.Ed from Herzog Academic College, and is currently finishing a master's in education at Herzog. Previously, Rabbi Schwartz served as the head rabbi of Bnei Akiva's Hachshara program for three and a half years. In addition, he teaches the writings of Rav Kook, Rebbe Nachman, Rav Shagar, Jewish philosophy, and Tanach at several yeshivot and midrashot in Jerusalem.